LET'S STUDY
2 PETER &
JUDE

Let's Study

2 PETER & JUDE

Mark G. Johnston

THE BANNER OF TRUTH TRUST

THE BANNER OF TRUTH TRUST

Head Office
3 Murrayfield Road
Edinburgh, EH12 6EL
UK

North America Office
610 Alexander Spring Road
Carlisle, PA 17015
USA

banneroftruth.org

© Mark Johnston 2005

First Published 2005
Reprinted 2012, 2023

ISBN

Print: 978 0 85151 917 3
Epub: 978 1 80040 362 8
Kindle: 978 1 80040 363 5

*

*

Typeset in 11/12.5 pt Ehrhardt MT by
Initial Typesetting Services,
Edinburgh.

Printed in the USA by
Versa Press, Inc.,
East Peoria, IL

FOR
BILLY AND IRENE
AND
JIM AND MAVIS

Contents

JUDE (continued)

Publisher's Preface

L *et's Study 2 Peter & Jude* is part of a series of books which seek to explain and apply the message of Scripture. The series is designed to meet a specific and important need in the church. While not technical commentaries, the volumes comment on the text of a biblical book; and, without being merely lists of practical applications, they are concerned with the ways in which the teaching of Scripture can affect and transform our lives today. Understanding the Bible's message and applying its teaching are the aims.

Like other volumes in the series, *Let's Study 2 Peter & Jude* seeks to combine explanation and application. Its concern is to be helpful to ordinary Christian people by encouraging them to understand the message of the Bible and apply it to their own lives. The reader in view is not the person who is interested in all the detailed questions which fascinate the scholar, although behind the writing of each study lies an appreciation for careful and detailed scholarship. The aim is exposition of Scripture written in the language of a friend, seated alongside you with an open Bible.

Let's Study 2 Peter & Jude is designed to be used in various contexts. It can be used simply as an aid for individual Bible study. Some may find it helpful to use in their devotions with husband or wife, or to read in the context of the whole family.

In order to make these studies more useful, not only for individual use but also for group study in Sunday School classes and home, church or college, study guide material will be found on pp. 111–126. Sometimes we come away frustrated rather than helped by group discussions. Frequently that is because we have been encouraged to discuss a passage of Scripture which we do not understand very well in the first place. Understanding must always be the foundation for enriching discussion and for thoughtful, practical application. Thus, in addition to the exposition of 2 Peter and Jude, the additional material provides questions to encourage personal thought and study, or to be used as discussion starters. The Group Study Guide divides the material into thirteen sections and provides direction for leading and participating in group study and discussion.

Foreword

It is all very well for someone to say, 'Let's study 2 Peter and Jude!' However, a prior question surely needs to be, 'Why study these books at all?' Given the fact that they have been both disputed and neglected in the Christian church from earliest times, what warrant do we have for urging people to read them and seek to grasp their message?

The answer in part is simply, 'Because they are in the Bible!' If God in his wisdom has seen fit to include these two little letters tucked away at the end of his written Word, then there must be good reason for it and we should make it our business to discover what that reason is. Even though there has been debate within the church at different points in history as to whether they actually belong in the canon of Holy Scripture (the collection of books that are recognized to be the breathed-out Word of God), the consensus of Christian thought has always been that they do belong in the canon. However, the fuller answer to our question lies in the message they contain and the circumstances in which they were written. We will come to those details in a moment, but suffice to say, Peter and Jude are both addressing problems that are a source of trouble to the church in every generation. These problems are subtle and dangerous because they arise from within the church – even the best of churches – as opposed to from outside the family of believers.

The letters serve as a warning to every healthy, stable congregation (and the Christians of whom they are comprised), calling them to be vigilant so that the blessings they enjoy are not undermined and destroyed without their realizing it. They also serve as an antidote to the kind of error that causes such damage, so that when we find ourselves in the midst of it, we have the ability to understand the false teaching and deal with it.

The tone of both letters may seem off-putting to some readers. Exposing false teachers and their teaching hardly comes across as something positive and uplifting; but it is a necessary part of God's message to his people. Elsewhere, Paul talks about the usefulness of Scripture and says that God has given it, not merely for Christians to be taught and trained in righteousness, but also reproved and corrected (*2 Tim.* 3:16). These are serious issues and they require serious consideration by all Christians and churches, regardless of their circumstances.

These pages are dedicated to two elders and their respective wives with whom I was privileged to serve in my first pastorate in Northern Ireland: Billy and Irene Wilson and Jim and Mavis Dixon. They were and continue to be very dear friends. I am grateful for their patience and encouragement in my early efforts to teach the message of these letters. Both couples have been an invaluable source of help and blessing to my wife and me – we will be forever in their debt.

Sincere thanks are also due to my present congregation: Grove Chapel, Camberwell, London. They have also heard a series of sermons on 2 Peter, albeit a more refined version of that which I had preached in Ireland. I am grateful to them in particular for granting me a period of study leave to work on the manuscript for this book.

It is only right that I also acknowledge how much I owe to Fiona, my wife, who has been my soul-mate and support for almost twenty-two years, to Lindsay, our special daughter with special needs, and to our son, Andrew, who played his own part in the production of these pages by asking me to preach on 2 Peter after reading it at camp.

The commentary that follows is based on the text of the English Standard Version of the Bible, though in places alternative translations will be offered to help bring out the meaning of particular passages more clearly.

MARK G. JOHNSTON
Grove Chapel, Camberwell
July 2005

Introduction

Before we can get down to a detailed study of the message of these two books, we need to make a number of preliminary comments that will help put their message in context. We do this not least because of the measure of controversy that has surrounded both books and the relationship they bear to one another. There is no shortage of material available dealing with these complex issues, but it is probably more helpful and constructive in the first place to focus on what is straightforward, namely the main themes they share.

PURPOSE AND THEMES

There is striking overlap between the messages of both letters. Both end with an exhortation to keep on growing in the faith (*2 Pet.* 3:18; *Jude* 20-21). Even though they are addressed to people who have been Christians for some time, they come as a reminder that all believers need to keep on growing spiritually. When we come to look at what is said on this theme in more detail – especially in Peter's letter – we will see that this means far more than accumulating knowledge; it means deepening our relationship with God through Jesus Christ.

The significance of this emphasis – again with Peter particularly in mind – should not be lost on us. Peter was the one disciple who always thought he knew the answers and who believed he could stand firm in any situation for Jesus. Yet it was Peter who discovered, in a very painful way, how immature and weak he really was. His letter, therefore, is a plea from the heart from someone who had to learn this lesson the hard way!

Peter's concern for *spiritual growth and maturity* dominates the first section of his letter. He begins by telling us what God has given us in Christ and why he has made such a provision for us who are Christians (*2 Pet.* 1:3–4). He then goes on to urge us to make full use of this divine provision (*2 Pet.* 1:5–11). The rest of the first chapter is taken up with a reminder of where all this can be found – in the gospel – and how we can be sure that the gospel's message is reliable and worthy of our trust (*2 Pet.* 1:12–21).

Jude's underlying concern was much the same. He speaks of his desire to write about 'our common salvation' (*Jude* 3), even though he appears to veer away from that purpose as he addresses the problem of false teachers within the church. However, in a round about way, he actually achieves his intention by showing that the gospel is central to everything in the Christian faith; not least its very survival in our own personal experience.

Both writers have much to say about *false teachers* and how to recognize them (*2 Pet.* 2:1–22; *Jude* 3–19). It is very clear in both cases that Peter and Jude's exposure of these people and their influence is not at all gratuitous or the kind of 'heresy hunting' that has sometimes characterized the church; rather, here is a vital matter of spiritual life and death. An essential part of Christian maturity is the ability to discern true from false – even when the church's spiritual leaders present it in biblical language. In both letters, the writers make it clear that we recognize such deviant teaching as much by the conduct of the teachers as by the content of their message.

The letters diverge most noticeably when it comes to the third major theme they share: *the return of Christ*. Peter takes up this theme in the last chapter of his letter (*2 Pet.* 3:1–18) and deals both with the nature of the second coming and its implications for how we are to prepare for it. Jude addresses it in much shorter compass, seeing the judgment that will coincide with Christ's return as a warning to those who waver in the faith (*Jude* 23) and as an encouragement to hold on to the One who in salvation first laid hold on us (*Jude* 22, 24–25).

All these themes have timeless relevance for the Christian church. They are not at all unrelated, but show how the strands of God's provision in redemption are carefully woven together. They also call us to understand what we are in Christ, so that we know how to live *in* him and *for* him until he returns.

AUTHORS AND DATES

Much of the dispute that has surrounded these books has centred upon the question of authorship. In the case of 2 Peter, it has been argued that the style and language of the letter is such that it bears little or no comparison to the other letter that bears Peter's name, or to the kind of man we know Peter to have been. The early church, it seems, was slow to recognize the place of this letter in the canon of Scripture – it was not clearly ascribed to Peter until the time of Origen in the third century – but this does not in itself warrant the rejection of the letter as authentic. Questions of authorship continued to rumble on through the time of the Reformation and even right down to the present.

Without minimizing the question of how we explain these difficulties, the letter itself gives ample evidence that Peter was indeed the author. He identifies himself in the opening verse (*2 Pet.* 1:1). He speaks very directly about himself (*2 Pet.* 1:12–15), claiming to be an eyewitness of the transfiguration of Jesus (*2 Pet.* 1:16–18). He also says that this letter is the second he has written to this group of readers (*2 Pet.* 3:1). There are many perfectly reasonable explanations for the apparent anomalies of language and style; these issues can be more fully explored in other, more technical, commentaries. As we have argued already in relation to the purpose behind the letter, the aims of the author could hardly be more fitting to a man like Peter who had walked this path already in his spiritual pilgrimage and had learned its lessons through his own bitter experience.

Turning to Jude we have a different problem on our hands: the question of Jude's identity. Peter may have been one of the best-known figures in the early church; but Jude, it seems, was one of the least! The name occurs only once in this form in the Bible (*Jude* 1), but it occurs many times both in its Hebrew form, 'Judah', and in its Greek equivalent, 'Judas'. But even narrowing it down to the Greek version, to whom does the name refer? The fact that he calls himself the 'brother of James' narrows the field further to two possibilities. Either this reference is to James the apostle who was martyred by Herod, or James the half-brother of Jesus who, more than likely, wrote the letter of James and who later led the church in Jerusalem after having worked in the surrounding area following the martyrdom of Stephen. The balance of opinion among Christian scholars leans towards the latter option, and the simple explanation for the abbreviated form of his name is that it avoids any confusion with Judas Iscariot.

If that is the case, then there is a strong argument for saying that the letter of Jude may be one of the earliest of the New Testament documents – written possibly as early as AD 40. However, there is no way of being certain about the date of the letter. The language and illustrations Jude uses would suggest that he is writing to Jewish converts who were familiar not only with the writings of the Hebrew Bible, but Jewish apocryphal writings as well. Once again, this would hint at an earlier rather than a later date for the letter's composition, putting it sometime before the Jewish Diaspora. Much of this is speculation, however, and the best we can say for certain is that it was probably written sometime between AD 40 and AD 80.

Establishing a date for 2 Peter is a little easier. It is clear from what he says that Peter knew his days were numbered and that his death was not far away (*2 Pet.* 1:12–15). If it is true, as the tradition of the early church suggests, that Peter was put to death during the reign of the Emperor Nero, then this letter must have been penned between AD 65 and AD 68. Although there are some details that have raised questions over whether or not the date should be earlier, locating it at this point in the history of the New Testament church would be consistent with issues that were widespread among the churches at that time.

LINKING JUDE WITH 2 PETER

It might seem a little odd at first to link two books of the New Testament that are not found in sequence in its traditional arrangement; yet they are linked together more often than not. The reason for this lies in the fact that there are some huge similarities between the two.

It is not merely that there is a significant degree of overlap between their main themes, but that the language and style is so similar as well. Out of twenty-five verses that make up the letter of Jude, fifteen are found in 2 Peter, either in their entirety or in part. Clearly there was some deliberate link intended since no attempt is made to mask the overlap.

There are three possibilities that might explain this connection. Jude could have drawn on Peter, Peter could have drawn on Jude, or both could have drawn on an independent source – possibly a tract that was written against false teachers around that time. The debate over these options has often been long and involved, but the easiest explanation would seem to be that Jude was written first. Then, because the issues it addressed were neither localized nor merely a passing phase, 2 Peter was written to expand Jude's message and give it a wider circulation in churches of a Gentile as well as a Jewish background.

We should neither be surprised nor alarmed by such 'borrowing' of material by biblical authors. We see many examples of it among Old Testament authors, in the way the Old Testament is frequently quoted and expounded by the New, and also in the way that New Testament writers, and even Jesus himself, are quite happy to duplicate material in different settings.

These background details set the scene and leave us free to look more closely at the message of 2 Peter and Jude in turn. As we do so, we will not only be stepping back in time into the world of the New Testament church, but very quickly learning that the issues our Christian forebears had to face are little different from the ones we face in the twenty-first-century church.

2 PETER

I

The Importance of Being Certain

Simeon Peter, a servant and apostle of Jesus Christ, to those who have obtained a faith of equal standing with ours by the righteousness of our God and Saviour Jesus Christ: ²May grace and peace be multiplied to you in the knowledge of God and of Jesus our Lord (2 Pet. 1:1–2).

Before we plunge into a detailed study of any book of the Bible, we need to pause on its threshold, as it were, and get our bearings. We need not only to look at the words with which we are greeted as we step into its world, but also to stop and breathe in the atmosphere of that world. We must try and step out of our own world into the world of those to whom Peter first wrote this letter.

For us twenty-first-century readers the immediate impact of Peter's opening words will be quite different from their impact on his original audience. It is not just that his choice of words and form of greeting would have been much more familiar to them, but these words also resonated with the circumstances Peter's fellow Christians were facing at that time. If we are to get to the heart of Peter's message from the outset, we need to hear his words as they are filtered through that first-century world.

When we do that, two things strike us. The first is that Peter was speaking to struggling Christians in a struggling church. While the

New Testament church had already begun to endure a major attack from outside its ranks, in the form of Jewish and Roman persecutions, it was also now facing a major attack from within. False teachers were twisting the message of the gospel and damaging the faith of those who had believed it. The combined effect of these attacks was a loss of certainty in the faith and of stability in the Christian life. The confidence of the churches was being seriously undermined.

Peter's response to that, therefore, right from the very start of his letter, is to stress the importance of being certain in the Christian life. Certainty is intimately bound up with stability. Peter will address our need to be certain of our standing before God, the reliability of the revealed message that comes from God – the very truth of God himself – and, finally, the claim that Jesus Christ will return in person at some point in the future.

We probably need to remember that the problem of doubt is one that increased as the New Testament era progressed. In the early days of New Testament Christianity there was an immediacy to the gospel message that was rooted in its proximity to the earthly life and work of Jesus Christ. The presence and testimony of many eyewitnesses of the gospel events served to bolster confidence, but as time passed and the gospel spread geographically, distance led to doubt. All this was compounded by the tendency in New Testament times to look for an imminent return of the Saviour – clearly an event for which the world is still waiting.

When we see the issues that these Christians were facing we begin to appreciate the timelessness of what Peter has to say. Doubt and instability have troubled the church through the ages and have become a particular problem in the social and intellectual climate of the world we live in today.

Peter addresses these issues from the very start of his letter. He points to our need for certainty – whether as those who are seeking God and exploring the Christian message for the first time, or as those who are already believers. This is true in three key areas.

THE MESSAGE OF SALVATION

Peter's opening words follow a standard form of greeting used as much in the secular world as in the Christian world of his day.

However, as with all the other apostolic writers, Peter was conscious that the words he wrote were not merely his own, but were from God, and with God there are no wasted words. So even the most ordinary and familiar words are loaded with an altogether different weight as God speaks into the situation his people face. Far from being a mere formality, these words of greeting are an integral part of the message itself.

So, as Peter introduces himself – especially as he sets out to deal with issues that lie at the heart of salvation – he wants to assure his readers that he really does have the authority to speak of such things. (If people think very carefully about whom they can trust with their personal finances, how much more carefully should they consider whom they can trust with the deepest needs of their souls!) Peter describes himself, therefore, in two ways: as 'a *servant* and *apostle* of Jesus Christ' (1:1). On both counts he is claiming an authority that is not his own.

In calling himself 'a servant' he is pointing to the fact that what he does is not done on his own initiative, but only at his Master's bidding. So, if his readers want to take issue with anything he says, they need to take the matter up with his Master, the Lord Jesus Christ, not with Peter the servant! Even though it is true that all Christians are Christ's servants, Peter and his fellow apostles were called to serve the Lord in a unique sense. They had been called and commissioned by Jesus in a very special way and had been told that they were to play a foundational role in establishing the New Testament church. Their very personal and direct relationship with Christ gave them a distinct authority – an authority not confined to their own lifetime in the first-century world, but to their writings throughout the whole of subsequent history.

However, when Peter also calls himself 'an apostle of Jesus Christ' he is raising his credentials to a higher and unique level. It is rather like those forms of identification which, when presented for inspection, are immediately recognized and accepted – no further questions need to be asked!

As with the designation 'servant', the word 'apostle' had a fairly wide application in New Testament Christianity. At its most basic level it could simply mean 'someone who is sent', or perhaps, 'someone who is sent with the gospel' – a kind of missionary. The word, however, was also used with a distinctive meaning when it came to the thirteen men who were to become the spiritual foundation stones of the New Testament church (*Eph.* 2:20). These men were specially qualified as those who had been with Christ and were eyewitnesses of his resurrection (*Acts* 1:21–22). There would have been no hesitation on the part of his first readers in realizing that Peter was using the word 'apostle' in its specialized sense.

Why was this important? Because any right-minded person would want to know why they should listen to an uneducated fisherman from the hill country of Galilee like Peter! The same is true for any-one as they open this book (and it is a perfectly understandable con-cern to raise). Peter is informing us that he has been given this special apostolic ministry literally by divine appointment. 'Simon Peter, a servant and apostle of Jesus Christ' – through these words Peter is presenting his credentials as God's messenger, before bringing God's message. We soon realize how important this is when we look at the contents of his message!

THE SOURCE OF SALVATION

One of the most damaging ways in which Christians have understood themselves and their experience has been the notion that there are two kinds of Christians and two kinds of Christian experience. This error has surfaced in various forms throughout history. In the early church there was a false distinction made between Christians converted from among the Jews and those converted as Gentiles. This was to be one of the major causes of controversy and division in the early days of the church. Later on, towards the end of the first century and well into the second, tensions grew between those who embraced a straightforward understanding of the gospel drawn from a plain reading of Scripture and those who claimed to possess some kind of deeper knowledge. This was to manifest itself in full-blown form in the so-called Gnostic movement. More recently the same kind of tensions have emerged over groups of Christians who have claimed a higher life, or a deeper insight, or a second experience of the Holy Spirit. The effect of such claims, of course, is to make many Christians feel as though their own personal experience of the faith is in some way inferior and that their status as Christians is only second-rate.

Peter is none too subtle in the way he addresses this particular issue in the next section of his greeting to his Christian readers. He describes them as 'those who have obtained a faith of equal standing with ours' (1:1). (He uses the word 'faith' here in the sense of the experience of believing, rather than of a body of truth to be believed.) Whatever these people may think about how their faith compares with that of other groups within the church, they should rest content in the knowledge that it is on a par with the faith of the apostles. There was nothing second-rate in what they had experienced!

How could they be sure of this? Because of the source from which that salvation had come. Their salvation – 'faith' – had come through the 'righteousness of our God and Saviour Jesus Christ' (1:1). Peter's choice of words harks back to the way Paul describes the essence of salvation in his letter to the Romans: it is the righteousness revealed in the gospel that is 'from God' and is 'by faith from first to last' (*Rom.* 1:17, NIV). The salvation God provides through the gospel of Christ comes with a cast-iron guarantee of authenticity. For the Christians of Peter's day it stood in stark contrast to the cheap and dangerous imitations that were being peddled among the churches.

If there is one thing that we need to be sure of when it comes to our hope of salvation, it is that we have not been deceived into embracing something that will not save us when we finally face God's judgment. In a sense, Peter is saying we should not judge by mere appearances. Even though there are many forms of spiritual experience that go under the name of 'Christianity', there is only one that is genuine. Just as we would check the genuineness of something we had bought by finding out from where it had come, so too with the message on which we rest our hopes of salvation. Only when we are sure that God is the source of our salvation and that it provides the righteousness we need for everlasting fellowship with him, can we rest assured that the salvation we have is the real thing.

THE KEY TO SALVATION

Once more, these opening words would have sounded very familiar to their original audience because they had been heard on numerous occasions: 'May grace and peace be multiplied to you in the knowledge of God and of Jesus our Lord' (1:2). Although Peter gives these well-known words a distinctly Christian flavour by linking them to Christ, they were still very much associated with the standard form of greeting used in the Greek and Roman world at that time. However, unlike correspondents who wished to convey a blessing from themselves, Peter is very deliberately communicating a blessing that comes from God through Jesus Christ, his Son. Yet again he takes familiar words and impregnates them with a richer and deeper meaning. He invokes the promise of God's favour ('grace') and prays for the believers' deepest personal well being ('peace'), to which God's favour leads.

In many ways these two words define most fully what salvation is all about. They speak of our standing with God and the good things we receive from him. Peter has already alluded to both of these in his opening salutation. The 'faith of equal standing with ours' that comes 'by the righteousness of our God and Saviour Jesus Christ' points to an experience of God's saving grace (what we receive from God) that brings peace through the justifying righteousness of Jesus Christ (our standing with God). But Peter is not content to see such experience merely in terms of what happens to us at the moment of our conversion. He prays for all his believing readers to experience this grace and peace experience may be 'multiplied' in their relationship with God.

We will see how Peter takes up this thought almost immediately as he moves into the main body of his letter's message. As with every relationship, a Christian's fellowship with God through Christ is one that needs to grow and mature. The blessings we experience at conversion are blessings yet to be experienced to the full. We must constantly press on towards this full experience of the grace and peace of God – using every means God provides – until 'filled with all the fullness of God' (*Eph.* 3:19) in the world to come.

Peter pinpoints the key to spiritual growth: 'the knowledge of God and of Jesus our Lord'. The letter's original readers would have detected that Peter's choice of the word 'knowledge' was by no means accidental. The advocates of the new spirituality, who were unsettling so many Christians at that time, also spoke about 'knowledge', but they had in mind the idea of a mystic knowledge that leads to a higher life. Peter, however, uses a Greek word that means something more than that. Indeed, what he had in mind goes beyond both mystic knowledge and even academic knowledge; it is instead a rich and personal knowledge. Or, to put it another way, it is an experience that grows out of genuine understanding. The Bible uses this kind of language somewhat euphemistically to speak of the sexual union between a man and a woman, but does so in a way that actually shows how the joy of such a union is found. Only as two people understand each other more fully will they enjoy their relationship more deeply.

The same is true in our experience of God in salvation (which the Bible delights to describe in terms of a spiritual marriage). Peter wants us to realize that the way a Christian enters more fully into the joy of what it means to be a Christian is not by means of unusual post-conversion experiences, but, rather, by growing in our understanding of and response to God. All this comes through growing in our love for Christ our Saviour. It is all about cultivating the relationship he has established with us by grace.

It would be naïve of us to think that there is such a thing as a Christian life free from doubt and uncertainty. But it would be even more naïve to think that God has not given us a gospel that addresses these doubts and uncertainties and answers them, not merely through what he has said, but in what he has done publicly and put on record historically for all to see. In a world in which our faith is often plagued by doubt, it is important that we are sure both of the God and of the gospel in which we have believed. That is the note Peter is sounding as he begins his second letter.

2

God's Great Provision for Our Greatest Need

His divine power has granted to us all things that pertain to life and godliness, through the knowledge of him who called us to his own glory and excellence, ⁴by which he has granted to us his precious and very great promises, so that through them you may become partakers of the divine nature, having escaped from the corruption that is in the world because of sinful desire (2 Pet. 1:3–4).

Peter is writing to people who are genuine Christians, but who are facing a serious crisis in their faith. It is fascinating, therefore, to see how he begins to address their situation as he moves from his opening greeting to the first main point in his letter.

It is worth noting that he does not focus immediately on the problems they were facing, but on the provision God has made for them. Nor does he tell the believers what they must do to overcome their difficulties. Instead he directs them to the spiritual resources from which they can draw what they need to live to the glory of God in this sinful world.

There is always a temptation to face our problems in the Christian life by looking downwards and inwards: to focus on our problems and difficulties, and to rummage through our own resources to find an answer to them. This tendency is reflected in the number of Christian books that are preoccupied with analysing problems and providing 'How to . . .' manuals to solve them. That is never the way God works as he addresses his children and their needs in his Word. Far from encouraging us to look down and in, he urges us to look up and out!

So Peter launches into the message that his troubled fellow Christians in their dispiriting circumstances so desperately needed to hear by reminding them of the gospel and how it accomplishes its work in the life of the believer. Peter's approach reminds us of the way in which the Christian message is radically different from that of every other religion. Other faiths proclaim what their devotees must do for their gods in order to find peace and security. Even some of the faiths that are related to the name 'Christian' effectively say the same thing. But that kind of message can never be called 'good news', because no matter how hard we try, or how much we do, we can never be sure that we have done enough to attain the desired goal. By total contrast, the message of the gospel – God's good news – is all about what he has done for us uniquely and completely through his Son, the Lord Jesus Christ.

The full force of what all of this means for us comes out in the two verses we want to consider in this chapter. In many ways verses 3 and 4 represent the distilled essence of the gospel. Because their content is so tightly packed and so powerfully stated, it is hard to fully fathom all that Peter is saying here. However, in order to grasp something of their meaning, it is no bad thing to trace the logic of what Peter says in reverse. When we do that, four things become clear.

WE ALL HAVE A GREAT NEED

In any closely reasoned argument, we often have to go to the conclusion at the very end in order to make sense of what is being said. That is very much the case in these two verses. In his greeting he has already put the spotlight on the faith and salvation that are ours in Christ, but here his focus is on the goal of that salvation. It is that, 'having escaped from the corruption that is in the world because of sinful desire', we 'become partakers of the divine nature' (1:4). This is God's great goal for his people – the meeting of a need that goes far deeper than any other we possess in this life. This goal is expressed both positively and negatively.

We will come back to Peter's positive assertion in a moment, but, first, let us think about what he means by the statement, 'having escaped from the corruption that is in the world because of sinful desire'. These Christians (who were overwhelmed by their many and varied problems and difficulties) actually have one underlying problem, which is the cause of all their other problems. This is 'the corruption that is in the world because of sinful desire'. Peter uses 'world' in the sense of a race that is in rebellion against God and under his righteous judgment as a result. In other words, there is not merely corruption around and about these Christians, but there is corruption also within them, and they need to escape from both the power and the consequences of it.

Translating this into our own experience, it is clear that we too may have many needs, but none is greater than the need to be rescued from a world that is ruined and rotting away. On the east coast of England there are many fine homes in what appear to be prime locations, set on magnificent cliff-tops, with panoramic sea views. However, severe coastal erosion is causing the very ground to crumble from under these 'dream homes' and soon they all will come crashing down into the sea. In the gospel, God calls us to look beyond life's immediate problems or pleasures to the larger horizon – our eternal destiny – and to examine the foundations on which we are building our lives in the present.

We can perhaps see clearly how this is true for the unbeliever; however, Peter is addressing Christian people in his letter. How can these words apply to Christians who have already been rescued? We must understand that the spirit of rebellion that infests the world is always infiltrating the church – not least through the influence of false teachers, whom we shall meet later in this letter. The apostle Paul describes this spirit of rebellion as the 'sin that dwells within me' (*Rom.* 7:20). The problem of indwelling sin faces every Christian and it will never be fully resolved so long as we are in this present world. Peter uses a tense for 'having escaped' that looks forward to the believer's final redemptive deliverance that will only take place when Christ returns and the perfection of the age to come arrives. Therein lies our ultimate need and there also we find the reason for Peter's longing – expressed at the end of the letter – for 'the day of God' to dawn (*2 Pet.* 3:12).

WE WERE ALL MADE FOR A GREAT DESTINY

If the negative expression of this deliverance were the sum total of a Christian's experience of salvation, we would be left with an image of believers on earth being little more than bedraggled survivors or castaways – rescued by the skin of their teeth, with very little left to live for. But that is not the case. Peter's assertion that we are rescued from a world that in many ways is like a sinking ship is only half the story. The gospel not only tells us what we are *saved from* through Christ; but, more significantly, what we are *saved for*. Hence we have this breathtaking statement: 'so that . . . you may become partakers of the divine nature' (1:4).

What do these words mean? Clearly Peter is not suggesting that Christian experience is like the kind of pantheistic mysticism common in his day and prevalent in present-day Buddhism and New Age spirituality; he is not teaching that the Christian becomes part of the being of God. Rather, he is restating God's original purpose and grand design for human beings at creation. Man was made in the image of God and was designed to exist and function in fellowship with his Creator. Peter is teaching us that it is only in union and communion with God through Jesus Christ that we can discover what it means to be truly human.

The fellowship man enjoyed with his God was lost through the Fall when Adam sinned and was driven, not merely from the garden of Eden, but from the presence of the Lord. But that perfect and unhindered fellowship will be perfectly restored for the Christian through the redeeming work of Jesus Christ. Again Peter is urging his readers to look beyond their present circumstances and, indeed, beyond the horizons of time, to the coming eternity and to the perfection it will usher in for those who live by faith in Christ.

But Peter's words also point us to the fact that this fellowship with God is something every Christian experiences in the here and now. It is ours at the moment of new birth when we are brought into union with Christ and it expresses itself in our daily communion with God through faith in Christ. So, in the midst of the pain and perplexity of their present circumstances, Peter is reminding these struggling Christians of their deep and precious bond with Christ, which nothing can ever destroy.

In the light of what Peter says, we are surely prompted to look around and within at the wreckage of humanity in this world – lives that are burdened and spirits that are crushed – and to ask ourselves, 'Is this really all there is to life?' The gospel's answer is a resounding

'No!' This was never the destiny God intended for the creatures he made to reflect his own glory. The gospel tells us that what we have been robbed of through Adam's sin and fall, God graciously restores through the saving work of the Second Adam, Jesus Christ. God's people are destined for the supreme glory of eternal union and communion with him.

WE HAVE BEEN GIVEN A GREAT SAVIOUR

As we trace these thoughts backwards into verse 3, we begin to feel the power of Peter's logic. Such a great deliverance and destiny as we see set out in the gospel of necessity demands a great Deliverer to secure it. That is exactly what Peter has in mind when he speaks of the One who 'called us to his own glory and excellence'. In other words, the 'grace and peace', found 'in the knowledge of God and of Jesus our Lord' (1:2) – the grace and peace of salvation – become ours as God the Father calls us out of our sin to himself through Jesus Christ his Son. His call to us opens our eyes to his glory and excellence, or goodness.

Peter may well have been thinking back to the time when Jesus called him to be his disciple. When Jesus began his earthly ministry, he appeared to be a very ordinary person – just the carpenter from Nazareth (*Mark* 6:3) – but it was not long before something extra-ordinary began to be seen in every detail of his life. There was a 'glory and excellence' about him – a glory that was bound up with his deity, and an excellence or goodness that was displayed especially through his teaching and miracles. So when Jesus issued the summons to Peter and his fellow fishermen to leave their nets and follow him (*Mark* 1:17–18), there was an irresistible attraction in the words of such a glorious person.

The big temptation facing the Christians to whom Peter was writing, floundering as they were in the internal struggles of church life, was to turn their eyes away from Jesus and focus on all their troubles instead. Peter, by turning them back to where their Christian life began, directs their attention to Jesus, showing him to be the One in whom the life of faith not only has its roots, but continues to grow. Peter reminds us that Christians are to always keep the eyes of their faith fixed on the glory and excellence of Jesus because it is his glory and excellence that set him apart as the only Saviour who is worthy of our trust.

WE HAVE IN CHRIST A GREAT SALVATION

Putting all this together, what do we get? 'His divine power has granted to us all things that pertain to life and godliness through the knowledge of him' (1:3). God supplies through Christ, not merely some of what we need for a true experience of his salvation (life and godliness), but *everything* that we need. Everything needful for eternal life and for living it out in daily experience is provided for us through our union with Christ. That being so, the promises God makes in the gospel are both 'precious and very great' (1:4)!

Once again Peter shows us the importance of 'knowledge'. God's power provides and his promises guarantee this great salvation through an intimate and personal relationship with his Son. Christ, therefore, is not only the means, but also the essence of salvation, because there is nothing provided in salvation that is apart from him. The more we know him, the more deeply we will share in the grace and strength we need to do God's will, which he alone supplies.

Grasping what this means helps us to understand the tension within these verses – a tension we often feel in our Christian lives – between the promise of the future and the painful realities of the present. There are times when we, like the first recipients of this letter, might be tempted to think that the promise of salvation is entirely confined to the future – that the gospel offers nothing more than 'pie-in-the-sky-when-we-die'. But Peter shows that this is not the case at all.

The thrust of his message in these verses is that all who believe in Christ have a present foretaste of the joys, blessings, and security of the world to come. God's power equips us with new life, a life that is bound up uniquely with Christ and fellowship with him. To be aware of this is an enormous comfort and encouragement, not only to the Christians to whom Peter was writing, but also to hard-pressed believers throughout the ages. As we feel the struggle of living in a spiritually hostile world, and of conflicting thoughts and feelings in our hearts, the remedy is not to get tangled up in either, but to look by faith to Jesus Christ who sets us free from both. In him we have a salvation that is complete, certain, and sure.

The words of the old chorus, though simple, have a profound ring of truth about them:

Turn your eyes upon Jesus,
Look full in his wonderful face;
And the things of earth will grow strangely dim,
In the light of his glory and grace.

Keep your eyes upon Jesus,
Let nobody else take his place;
So that, hour by hour, you may prove his power;
Till at last you have run the straight race.

There could hardly be a simpler, or sweeter summary of what Peter says we as Christians ought to know!

3

Finding Certainty in Life

*For this very reason, make every effort to supplement your faith
with virtue, and virtue with knowledge, ⁶and knowledge with
self-control, and self-control with steadfastness, and
steadfastness with godliness, ⁷and godliness with brotherly
affection, and brotherly affection with love. ⁸For if these
qualities are yours and are increasing, they keep you from being
ineffective or unfruitful in the knowledge of our Lord Jesus
Christ. ⁹For whoever lacks these qualities is so short-sighted that
he is blind, having forgotten that he was cleansed from his
former sins. ¹⁰Therefore, brothers, be all the more diligent to
make your calling and election sure, for if you practise these
qualities you will never fall. ¹¹For in this way there will be
richly provided for you an entrance into the eternal kingdom
of our Lord and Saviour Jesus Christ (2 Pet. 1:5–11).*

One of the great pleasures of parenthood is to watch our children
grow up and, as they do so, to see them become more and more
confident and self-assured. We want them to mature! The same is
true for those who are spiritual 'fathers in the faith' – they too long
for their spiritual children to grow towards maturity and stability.
That is what Paul expresses in his blueprint for healthy church life
(*Eph.* 4:11–16) and what the ageing apostle John delights in, when
he says, 'I have no greater joy than to hear that my children are
walking in the truth' (*3 John* 4). This is certainly Peter's great
concern in his letter to his fellow Christians: in many ways they were
still in their spiritual infancy, yet facing situations that tested their
faith to the extreme.

[15]

His primary concern for them is that they should find certainty in the faith (1:10). This is why he exhorts them to press on towards spiritual maturity in every aspect of their lives. We have already noted that Peter begins his letter by laying the foundation for certainty in the objective truth of the gospel (1:1–4). Now he shifts his focus to the process of working that certainty out in our personal Christian experience.

Again there are similarities between Peter's exhortation to the members of the family of God and our experience of life in our natural families. It is possible for a parent to show a child what it means to be mature – the father or mother can act as an objective role model to the child. But a nurturing process is also needed if the child is to become a stable grown-up person. Maturity is something they must make their own. So here Peter spells out what is involved in nurturing Christians towards maturity and stability in their personal spiritual lives.

The issues here are of timeless relevance to every generation in the church; but perhaps especially (strange though it may seem) to those who are not under pressure. When things are 'going well' in the Christian life, it is all too easy to become complacent and allow the great certainties of the Christian faith to sit loosely to us. But when that is not so, and crises arise, suddenly our faith collapses, because we have not married together the objective truth of the gospel and a subjective certainty in our faith in the gospel. It has often been proved true throughout the history of the church that Christians under pressure have thrived spiritually and been the most vibrant and effective ambassadors of Christ.

With these considerations in mind Peter spells out for us the vital importance of progress and growth for the Christian. We cannot afford to stay at the baby stage of spiritual development. He shows not only the need for growth, but also where that growth leads, and how to cultivate it in our personal experience.

THE INGREDIENTS OF SPIRITUAL GROWTH

Nothing grows in a vacuum – seeds need soil – so Peter is careful to root what he says about the ingredients of spiritual growth in the soil of God's grace. The 'For this very reason . . . ' (1:5) that introduces this section links all that it contains to the preceding verses. It is only because God in his grace has given us 'everything we need for life and godliness' (1:3, NIV), that we are able to make use of those God-given resources to cultivate spiritual growth in our lives. Indeed, when we begin to appreciate how great these resources actually are, we realize how great is our responsibility to make full use of them. Every Christian ought to be energetic and enthusiastic in his or her pursuit of progress in the faith.

Straight away this stops us in our tracks. All too often we grumble and complain about our lack of progress and begin to feel that we need something more – hence the attraction of some kind of secondary spiritual life-experience, the offer of which so many Christians find irresistible. But the implication of what Peter is saying is that *we do not need something extra*. In Christ's gospel everything we need is ours already. What we really need is to make use of what we have. It is rather like having a high-tech computer, camera, or some other piece of equipment. Most people use only a small percentage of its potential, because they do not realize just how much it is capable of doing. God has placed enormous spiritual potential in each of his children and it is only as they put it to the test through faith and obedience that they will discover what that potential can achieve.

So Peter is calling us to action in these verses. We are to 'make every effort' to cultivate in our lives the range of Christian graces he is about to list. In the same way that the new converts in the Jerusalem church made astounding progress in the faith because 'they devoted themselves' to the means of grace (*Acts* 2:42), so must we. What Paul wrote to the believers in Philippi – 'work out your own salvation with fear and trembling, for it is God who works in you' (*Phil.* 2:12–13) – is true for all Christians in all places. We must make full use of all the resources God has graciously put at our disposal in Christ.

What, then, are the ingredients for spiritual growth that we are to stir into our lives? Peter lists eight for us. It is not an exhaustive list; but it is a representative sample of the key characteristics of a healthy and effective Christian life.

He begins with 'faith' (1:5). By that he means personal faith, or trust in God (as opposed to 'the faith' – the body of truth encompassed in the gospel). We cannot cultivate genuine spiritual experience without genuine saving faith in Christ. We cannot go on with God unless we first begin with him; but, having begun, we cannot stand still; we need to make progress.

In the first place, therefore, Peter tells his readers, 'make every effort to supplement your faith with virtue' (1:5). He uses the same word that is translated 'excellence' in verse 3. Since he uses it there in relation to Jesus, this gives us some idea of what he has in mind in terms of Christian character. God wants us to be Christlike as his children! We must seek to mirror him in our thoughts, words, and deeds.

The next characteristic in the list is 'knowledge' (1:5). Even though this sounds like the word already used in connection with our experience of God's blessings in the gospel (1:2–3), actually a different Greek word is used in this verse. Here Peter is referring to practical wisdom or discernment. This is the kind of knowledge that will have an impact on how we live.

He then speaks of the need for 'self-control' (1:6). It is not hard to detect a certain logical progression in the traits listed. Christians who are controlled by a discerning knowledge, instead of passion and instinct, will experience a 'self-mastery' that will mark them out as strikingly different from the average man or woman of the world. The Christian's life has inbuilt constraints that flow directly from Christ's lordship over him or her.

Self-control is followed by 'steadfastness', or perseverance (1:6). This is the idea of being unmoved or undeterred by difficulty or distress. If self-control has to do with our response to the allure of illicit pleasures, then steadfastness relates to our response to uninvited pain. It is all about the Christian coping under pressure.

Then comes 'godliness' (1:7) – reverence or piety which grows out of a life lived with a deep awareness of always being in the presence of God. This is not merely a fatalistic sense of God, which many people share. Rather it is a son's awareness of being in his Father's family, under his care and in rich communion with him. Godliness grows out of being deeply conscious of this one relationship that colours and shapes all others.

This reverent relationship with God in turn flows into a loving relationship with other members of God's family. The church of Christ, the family of God, ought to be characterized by 'brotherly affection' (1:7). Here Peter uses the Greek word *philadelphia* – the kind of love that binds a family together. Peter is applying the words he heard Jesus speak to his disciples: 'Love one another, just as I have loved you' (*John* 13:34).

All of this blossoms, finally, into 'love' – *agape* – that special Greek word the New Testament writers used so much (1:7). This is the unique love God has for his people – a love that spills over into their love for one another and even for the world in all its spiritual need.

What happens when ingredients for a cake are spread on a table? In one sense they might look rather bland and unappealing; but when they are blended and baked together they are transformed into something of great beauty and delight. So it is with the spiritual ingredients outlined here by Peter. As a mere list they can seem a little nondescript, but when they are stirred into the lives of God's children we see his antidote for the kind of lacklustre Christianity that is all too often the norm. Here are the characteristics of the life every Christian ought to pursue with a passion!

THE IMPACT OF SPIRITUAL GROWTH

If we are in any doubt about the value of cultivating such Christian virtues in our lives, Peter forcefully presses home their worth. 'For if these qualities are yours and are increasing, they keep you from being ineffective or unfruitful in the knowledge of our Lord Jesus Christ' (1:8). In saying this, Peter is flagging up the warning that it is possible to be a Christian and yet live ineffectively and unfruitfully – to have a faith that makes little or no impact on the world around us.

We can perhaps see this principle illustrated in church history in the way that the lives of some Christians have so stood out that they have shown up the ineffectiveness and unfruitfulness of others by comparison. J. I. Packer makes just that point about the Puritans in his introduction to his book *Among God's Giants*.

> As Redwoods attract the eye, because they overtop other trees, so the mature holiness and fortitude of the great Puritans shine before us as a kind of beacon light, overtopping the stature of the majority of Christians in most

eras, and certainly so in this age of crushing urban collec-
tivism, when Western Christians sometimes feel and often
look like ants on an anthill and puppets on a string . . . In
this situation the teaching and example of the Puritan giants
has much to say to us.[1]

It can only be dishonouring to God and distressing for ourselves to
profess to be Christians, yet have people look at us and say, 'So what?'
The seriousness of this sad phenomenon is not only to be judged in
terms of the implications for our Christian witness to the world, but
in terms also of our impact on the next generation of professing
Christians within the church. Ineffectiveness in one generation will
breed ineffectiveness in the next.

Peter feels this seriousness keenly, and so repeats what he has said,
only this time with a negative slant and a word of warning. He says,
'For whoever lacks these qualities is so short-sighted that he is blind,
having forgotten that he was cleansed from his former sins' (1:9).
He seems to use an unusual form of words – one that is intended to
touch a raw nerve among the erring churches of his day. The word
translated 'short-sighted' can also mean 'with closed eyes' and carries
the sense of a deliberate action – the shutting of one's eyes. In other
words, the problems these Christians were experiencing were as
much the fruit of wilful ignorance on their part, as to factors totally
beyond their control.

How many professing Christians are there today who have tasted
the privileges and power of the gospel, but have deliberately closed
their eyes to the demands of discipleship it makes on them? There is
much truth in the old adage, 'There are none so blind as those who
will not see.' The privilege of being taught by God carries with it the
responsibility of consciously living in the light of all we have learned
– that is the key to real and ongoing growth in the Christian life.

THE IMPORTANCE OF SPIRITUAL GROWTH

All of this is pressed home with sobering urgency in the closing
paragraph of this section. It is couched in words of encouragement;

---

[1]J. I. Packer, *Among God's Giants* (Eastbourne: Kingsway, 1991), pp. 11–12.

but carries an unspoken warning that is all too apparent. 'Therefore, brothers, be all the more diligent to make your calling and election sure' (1:10). In days when there were many who were professing faith, but whose faith was spurious, and days when there seemed to be an abundance of false teachers abroad, nothing could be more vital for Christians than to be sure that the faith they had embraced was the real thing.

Peter deliberately uses language that traces the roots of salvation right back to God and his eternal plan of redemption. He speaks of God's sovereign choice of a people for himself in eternity and the effectual call that brought that choice to fulfilment in history.

Given the confusion there has been among Christians over this issue, it is significant to notice that Peter is able to talk about such things without either denying or obscuring the exercise of our own wills in this matter. The God who chooses and calls his people requires a conscious and active response on their part. He does not believe for them; rather he, by his gracious workings in their lives, enables them to believe truly. So, given the divine enabling that is guaranteed in God's choice and imparted in his call, it is incumbent on us to be 'all the more diligent' to ensure that real saving grace is ours.

What does that mean in practice? In part it means never being content with spiritual complacency or apathy. Carelessness in matters of the soul is the mortal enemy of genuine assurance of salvation. It also means dealing with doubt. Whatever its source – whether intellectual doubts about the message of the Bible, or personal doubts about the genuineness of our faith – we need to address them and do all in our power to deal with them. One might well ask, 'How can you know if you are elect?' – a perfectly reasonable question to ask, since the names of those whom God has chosen are not disclosed to us in this world. However, the elect can be known by their coming to faith in Christ (*1 Thess.* 1:4–10). So, in answer to the question, 'How do I know I am elect?' I need to ask another: 'Have I put my faith in Jesus?'

Peter says if Christians pursue this certainty, two things will happen: first, they 'will never fall' (1:11) – not in the sense of falling from grace and losing their salvation, but of falling irrevocably into the kind of error and spiritual uselessness that was all too common at that time. Then, second, he can assure them that 'there will be richly provided for you an entrance into the eternal kingdom of our Lord and Saviour Jesus Christ' (1:12). All the struggles of 'going the distance' in the life of faith in a world that is hostile to God and to the gospel will pale into insignificance in the light of the welcome we will receive into God's everlasting kingdom in heaven.

When we start to grasp what Peter is saying, we realize that these great truths touch absolutely everything in our lives: what we value, how we seek to reach a fallen world, what we leave for our children, what we are looking forward to most of all, etc. Yet, how easy it is to sacrifice all these things on the altar of self-interest and the desire for immediate gratification in this present evil world. The new life given to us in Christ is one that transforms our present because it has transformed our future destiny.

A passage like this makes us stop and ask ourselves, not merely 'Have I got faith?' but, 'Am I sure the faith I claim to have is real?' If the answer is 'Yes' to both questions, then we need to ask to what extent we are using our privileges and fulfilling our responsibilities to the full.

4

Our Reasonable Faith

Therefore I intend always to remind you of these qualities, though you know them and are established in the truth that you have. ^{13}*I think it right, as long as I am in this body, to stir you up by way of reminder,* ^{14}*since I know that the putting off of my body will be soon, as our Lord Jesus Christ made clear to me.* ^{15}*And I will make every effort so that after my departure you may be able at any time to recall these things.* ^{16}*For we did not follow cleverly devised myths when we made known to you the power and coming of our Lord Jesus Christ, but we were eyewitnesses of his majesty.* ^{17}*For when he received honour and glory from God the Father, and the voice was borne to him by the Majestic Glory, "This is my beloved Son, with whom I am well pleased,"* ^{18}*we ourselves heard this very voice borne from heaven, for we were with him on the holy mountain.* ^{19}*And we have something more sure, the prophetic word, to which you will do well to pay attention as to a lamp shining in a dark place, until the day dawns and the morning star rises in your hearts,* ^{20}*knowing this first of all, that no prophecy of Scripture comes from someone's own interpretation.* ^{21}*For no prophecy was ever produced by the will of man, but men spoke from God as they were carried along by the Holy Spirit* (2 Pet. 1:12–21).

F ew things can feel more damaging to our personal faith than to hear someone saying to us, 'But that is just your opinion!' Yet that is precisely how many unbelievers dismiss our Christian testimony today. Even though their attitude towards the gospel may seem very 'post-modern' to us, it is interesting to note that it is anything but novel. From as far back as New Testament times there have been repeated attempts to neutralize the gospel message by portraying it as merely the private opinion of an over-zealous religious minority.

That was one of the major issues facing the church in Peter's day – hence his vigorous defence against the allegation that the apostolic message was a 'myth' (1:16). It may well have been the false prophets and teachers who levelled this charge against the apostles in an attempt to conceal the fact that their own message owed more to human speculation than divine revelation. Certainly it is often the case that the claim, 'God told me . . . !', can sound very pious and persuasive, and yet be nothing more than a smokescreen for personal opinion dressed up in prophetic language. When such claims are made, they inevitably divert attention away from the written Word of God and have the effect of destabilizing the faith of weak Christians.

Peter responds to this allegation that the gospel is a myth by urging his readers to pursue genuine certainty in their faith. They cannot afford to settle for anything less than a rock-solid foundation on which to place their trust concerning these most important issues of life. The only sure foundation is found in the Bible. He wants us to grasp the fact that the Christian faith is a reasonable faith – it is not a blind leap in the dark, but a step into the light – the glorious light of all that God has spoken and accomplished, verified for all to see in his Word.

In this section Peter's main teaching point is that the certainty we need in our faith cannot be separated from the certainty we find in God's Word. He explains what this means and reasons out its implications as he develops his case.

CERTAINTY COMES THROUGH BEING ESTABLISHED IN THE TRUTH

It is clear from what Peter says that he is not casting doubt on his readers' conversion experience. He is well aware of the fact that they know these things and are firmly established in them already (1:12). Nevertheless, he repeatedly reminds them of basic truths because they are of such foundational importance.

Three times in these verses he insists on drawing their attention back to doctrines which lie at the very heart of genuine Christian experience. (This in itself says something about the way one should teach the Christian faith and the role of repetition in that process.) Peter does this in part because these doctrines comprise the very essence of what the Christian faith is. In fact he describes them as 'the truth' in which they are established (1:12). In conversion, these people had put their faith in a message that claimed to be the truth. If that claim was false, then their faith was ill-founded and would not be able to deliver the salvation they sought.

The second reason why Peter makes no apology for reminding his readers of these things is that ' . . . I know that the putting off of my body will be soon' (1:14). He is clearly speaking about his impending death: for reasons not made entirely clear to us, Peter knew that he did not have much longer to live.

That being the case, he proceeds to give us a third reason why he was not embarrassed to repeat the basic doctrines of his teaching: he says, 'I will make every effort so that after my departure you may be able at any time to recall these things' (1:15). To be able to recall the apostle's words accurately after his death, his readers – both then and now – would need a written record which faithfully preserved the apostolic testimony to Jesus.

It is important for us to grasp why Peter emphasizes this point. Only the truth of the gospel is able to provide a salvation that is both real and lasting. His first-century readers were dangerously exposed to plausible sounding messages which were masquerading as truth. But a false gospel, no matter how plausibly presented, cannot save; only the true gospel saves. This is why Peter is at such pains to underscore the truth in these verses.

Some years ago, when I was trainee pilot, I had to undergo re-peated safety drills every time I sat in the cockpit of a plane. This was a vital part of my training, which was designed to prepare me to react in the proper manner in any mid-air crisis. The things that mattered most in flight safety became second nature to me through my repeated exposure to them in the safety drills. If faced with an emergency my training would enable me to respond in a way that would ensure a safe landing. So it is with the emergencies we face in the life of faith. It is only as we are drilled in the core truths of the gospel that we will avoid those tailspins of doubt that are so un-nerving and damaging to our faith.

No matter how long a person may have been a Christian, they are never too old to be reminded of certain basic truths. That is the reason Jesus gave the church an *aide-mémoire* in the form of the Lord's Supper. Again and again, as he calls his people round his table he reminds them of the bedrock of their salvation, not only in what God has said, but also in what he has accomplished through Jesus' death on the cross.

It is an issue of the utmost importance in the Christian life. What does your faith rest on – instinct and intuitio, or truth that can really be trusted? It is only as we are increasingly established in the truth of the gospel that we find the kind of certainty we need to persevere in the faith.

TRUTH THAT GIVES CERTAINTY RESTS ON EYEWITNESS TESTIMONY

Pontius Pilate famously asked the question, 'What is truth?' (*John* 18:38). It is the question that countless millions of people ask in all sorts of different contexts and for all kinds of reasons – often with the same note of cynicism that tinged Pilate's question.

There is, of course, a deep and philosophical side to this question which lies outside the limits of human knowledge and reason. But there is also an answer to it which is found within those limits: truth is what can be proved to be real, and to have actually happened – it is verifiable fact. It is that which has been said and done, and which has been personally witnessed and corroborated.

So Peter answers those who were undermining the apostolic message and unsettling the faith of many in the church by stating categorically, 'We did not follow cleverly devised myths when we made known to you the power and coming of our Lord Jesus Christ, but we were eyewitnesses of his majesty' (1:16). Even though much of what he saw and describes here as literally, 'the powerful coming of the Lord' seemed incredible – not least Jesus' claim to be God – yet this is what he and all his fellow-apostles saw and heard. They were eyewitnesses who had given their solemn testimony concerning these marvellous and historical events.

This is one of the most striking things about the character of the Christian gospel: it consists largely of testimony to what people saw and heard. As Paul said when on trial before Festus and Agrippa, 'This has not been done in a corner' (*Acts* 26:26). Indeed, Luke records that the apostolic testimony was frequently cross-examined in the courts of law – before Jewish courts, Roman courts, and ultimately the imperial Supreme Court in Rome. The apostles' testimony was put under intense legal scrutiny at a time when it would have been very easy for their enemies to show it to be false. The apostles' testimony was scrutinized and was found to be true.

Peter focuses his attention on one particular incident – he, James and John were with Jesus on the mountain when he was transfigured before them. They not only saw this extraordinary transfiguration, but also heard the voice of God declare the true identity of Jesus (1:17–18). It was the kind of incident that would have raised many an eyebrow, but here were three men who simply spoke of what they had seen and heard.

All kinds of claims and ideas are circulated in the name of 'truth', but when they are subjected to scrutiny, they prove to be false. What are we called to entrust ourselves to in the gospel? Truth that has been verified by countless witnesses – many of whom were willing to die rather than deny what they had clearly seen and heard. Only a faith soundly based on such tried and tested truth-claims can survive the attacks of enemies from the outside, and the corruption of sin from within. This is what we need and this is what the gospel of Jesus Christ supplies.

EYEWITNESS TESTIMONY CONFIRMS GOD'S SPIRIT-GIVEN WORD

However, Peter does not stop here. He presses home the implications of the apostles' testimony by linking it to the larger message of God's revealed and written Word in the Old Testament Scriptures. He says, 'And we have something more sure, the prophetic word' (1:19). He is referring to the testimony of the Old Testament which pointed to the coming of Christ. The Old Testament Scriptures have been authenticated and confirmed by all that has happened, by way of fulfilment, in the birth, life, ministry, death, and resurrection of Jesus Christ.

Peter now spells out the implications of what he has just said: 'You will do well to pay attention [to this Word] as to a lamp shining in a dark place, until the day dawns and the morning star rises in your hearts.' In this world, the only reliable guide for God's people is the revealed and written Word of God – the Bible. The qualification, 'until the day dawns and the morning star rises in your hearts', seems to be a reference to the day of Christ's return. On that day what has been acknowledged as objective truth in history will be personally experienced to the full as eternity begins to unfold.

The section closes with a climactic statement that refers not only to the testimony of the apostles but also to the Bible itself. 'Above all, you must understand that no prophecy of Scripture came about by the prophet's own interpretation. For prophecy never had its origin in the will of man, but men spoke from God as they were carried along by the Holy Spirit' (1:20–21, NIV).

Peter is speaking here about something that is of paramount importance – as he emphasizes when says, 'Above all, you must understand . . .' Our grasp of the uniqueness of the Bible is intimately bound up with our assurance of salvation and stability in the faith. We are called to place our faith, not in the flimsy words of men, but in God's infallible Word.

Peter goes on to describe the mysterious and extraordinary way in which the words of God came to be written down in what we now know as 'Scripture' (verse 20). When he says that these men, who spoke from God, were '*carried along* by the Holy Spirit', he uses the same word that is used of a ship being carried along as the wind fills its sails. The ship does not move by itself; it is driven along by the wind. These prophets did not speak their own words, of their own accord, but spoke the words of God, by the power of the Spirit of God.

In making this bold assertion, and linking the words of the apostles with the Word of God in Scripture, Peter was deliberately throwing down the gauntlet to the false teachers who were troubling the church. Could the same be said of them and their message? Would they dare to claim that they spoke from God, as they were carried along by the Holy Spirit?

The note Peter has sounded repeatedly in this section is one of warning to Christians. Do not yield to the temptation to let instinct and intuition lead you in your Christian life. Moreover, do not be deceived by those who deliver spine-tingling messages that purport to come directly from God. Both of these temptations are still very common and, if yielded to, will blow Christians and churches badly off course. How are we to meet such temptations? By giving our full attention to the Scriptures and asking ourselves such questions as: 'Is this doctrine found in the Bible?' 'Does this course of action tally with God's revealed and written Word?' If it does not, then pay no heed to it!

The beautiful thing about the Christian faith is that it can thrive under the most intense scrutiny. It is not afraid of being tested because, when it is, it proves to be what it claims to be – the truth of God that cannot be shaken!

5

A Clear and Present Danger

But false prophets also arose among the people, just as there will be false teachers among you, who will secretly bring in destructive heresies, even denying the Master who bought them, bringing upon themselves swift destruction. ²And many will follow their sensuality, and because of them the way of truth will be blasphemed. ³And in their greed they will exploit you with false words. Their condemnation from long ago is not idle, and their destruction is not asleep (2 Pet. 2:1–3).

It is amazing how lax we can be about threats and dangers in life – that is, at least until they suddenly land on our doorstep. We have seen it again and again with the threat of terrorism and drugs. Communities, and even entire nations, have been quietly complacent and unprepared until it is suddenly too late. Hence the expression – 'a clear and present danger' – coined by American politicians intent on warning people of such real threats. Some things may not seem sinister to us at first glance, but on closer inspection they may in fact be very dangerous.

The same has often been true in the church. Christians can be incredibly complacent over issues which pose a serious threat to the doctrinal integrity and the spiritual stability of the church. Very often it is only when the damage has been done that Christians see the danger! While it is true that in Christian love we are called to believe the best about our fellow Christians – especially those who teach us – we are at the same time called to 'test the spirits to see whether they are from God' (*1 John* 4:1). Christian love is never to be gullible; it is always to be tempered by shrewdness.

These are the issues Peter addresses at the beginning of this second chapter. He seeks to shake the Christians of his day out of their naïve complacency and alert them to a 'clear and present danger' within their own churches. The church was in danger from false teachers who were spreading their influence throughout the various congregations that existed at that time. But as with many Christians of more modern times such false teachers were too often seen as 'someone else's problem, not ours'. However, one by one, the churches were painfully discovering that the problem of false doctrine *was* their problem.

How can people be made to treat false teachers with the seriousness that they deserve? Only by exposing them for what they really are. That is what Peter does here. He makes four points about them.

THEY ARE PERVASIVE

This second chapter starts in a way that is seamlessly connected to the end of the first. However, the focus now shifts from the past to the present. Peter has been talking at length about the legacy of the true prophets of God in the Old Testament; now he goes on to speak of false prophets. In Old Testament times 'false prophets . . . arose among the people' and Peter says that 'there will be false teachers among you' as well (2:1).

Christians sometimes wonder why we need to have an interest in church history. The reason is because the issues faced by previous generations of Christians have a nasty habit of recurring. It is not merely in the world of fashion that it can be said, 'Whatever goes around, comes around'!

What makes many of these issues so serious is that they affect our understanding of the gospel and what it means to be a Christian. So, here, Peter makes it clear that the only true foundation for saving faith is the revealed and written Word of God – the Bible. Christians need to be able to discern what the revelation of God looks like. That is why Peter has taken the trouble, not only to spell out the characteristics of the true and saving revelation of God in the Old Testament Scriptures, but also to warn of the presence of false prophets in his day, when God's true apostles were bringing to light his New Testament revelation.

The Old Testament records the appearance of many false prophets and the clashes that took place between them and the true prophets of the Lord. Think of the high-profile and very public exchanges that occurred between Elijah and the prophets of Baal (*1 Kings* 18:16–40), Micaiah and Zedekiah (*1 Kings* 22:1–28), or Jeremiah and the lying prophets in the last days of the kingdom of Judah (*Jer.* 23:9–40). The presence of false prophets among God's people was a pervasive problem then, and continues to be so down to the present day.

Peter says that just as these false prophets 'arose' in the past, so 'there will be false teachers among you'. He does not say, 'there might be', or 'there could be', but 'there will be' such people at work in the church. (The shift in terminology from 'prophets' to 'teachers' indicates that the two are synonymous and refer to those who claim to speak in God's name.)

Even a cursory glance at New Testament Scriptures or subsequent church history serves to confirm Peter's prophetic warning. No generation is exempt from the dangers of such an evil influence. How, then, should we react? By taking Peter's warning seriously and realizing that false doctrine is an issue every Christian must face. We all need to cultivate a spirit of discernment in how we hear and respond to those who claim to teach God's Word. Like the Bereans of Paul's day, we need to examine the Scriptures to see if what is being taught is consistent with what God has said in his Word (*Acts* 17:11).

THEY ARE DESTRUCTIVE

As Peter goes on to describe the false teachers and the kind of influence they were exerting, he makes it clear why we need to be concerned about them. He says, they 'will secretly bring in destructive heresies' (2:1). Peter's words are shocking and it is tempting to think that such false teaching must be so blatantly obvious that it should be possible for us to spot it a mile off and avoid it like the plague. However, to think like that would be a mistake. The very real danger of false teaching lies in its subtlety. False teaching is sophisticated and difficult to detect, requiring Christians to be always on their guard.

It is easy for us to point to the very public controversies and failures of other churches with a sense of smugness, imagining that we are safe and immune from such confusion; but no church is safe from this threat. No church is immune from the kind of beguiling infiltration that will lead people astray and plunge congregations of Christian people into ruin.

That comes out in the fact that Peter calls this kind of teaching 'heresy' – a New Testament word that originally meant 'variant', or 'alternative'. If the course plotted by a ship's captain is inaccurate by just one degree at the start of an ocean voyage, the ship will never reach the intended destination. Indeed, before it has sailed very far it will be many miles off course!

The Bible makes it clear that there is latitude for interpretation in many areas of the Christian life. But it also teaches that certain doctrines are 'of first importance' (*1 Cor.* 15:3), concerning which there is no room for manoeuvre. Any kind of deviation in these teachings leads to spiritual destruction. Although we might be inclined to narrow the field of such teachings to what are sometimes called 'gospel truths', their scope is actually much wider than we think, because there are many teachings in Scripture that are bound up with the gospel and how it transforms our lives.

That seems to be the reason why Peter qualifies this statement with the words, 'even denying the Master who bought them, bringing upon themselves swift destruction' (2:1). In other words, there was an enormous contradiction between what the false teachers were saying with their lips and with their lives: a contradiction that brought shame and dishonour on the name of Jesus. Any teaching that fails to acknowledge the lordship of Christ over all of life is out of step with the kind of salvation promised in the gospel.

When we set out on a journey and choose to follow a certain road, we ought to be concerned not only about where that road begins, but also about where it ends. Nowhere is this more important than in the way of faith. Peter wants to warn us about certain teachers to whose doctrines we may feel drawn. Avoid them: their way will not lead you finally to Christ, but far away from him.

THEY ARE ATTRACTIVE

Peter highlights the appeal of such teachers and the subtlety of their teaching by telling us that there will not merely be some, but 'many' who 'will follow their sensuality' (2:2). There is something about their message that scores highly in the popular opinion polls. It has been a staggering fact throughout the history of the church that it does not take much to deflect large numbers of Christians off course, and almost always for the reasons Peter spells out here. He speaks of 'their sensuality' – that element in both the message and lifestyle of the false teachers that appeals to our human feelings, desires, and appetites.

Again, one might be inclined to read the word Peter uses and to think of sensuality in its most extreme and excessive forms – sexual licence and materialistic greed – and acknowledge that there have indeed been some glaring examples of such excess in the Christian church. But the apostle is alerting his Christian readers to something that is closer to their own everyday experience than one might care to admit. Peter is talking about that approach to teaching that by-passes the mind and goes straight to the senses – an approach that is more concerned with feeling good, than finding truth. (We must not forget that Peter has already stressed the vital link between being established in the truth and being stable in the faith, *2 Pet.* 1:12–15). When we see his warning in this light, we can appreciate just how insidious the allure of such false teaching actually is. It lulls its hearers into a pleasant complacency before leading them off into an outright denial of gospel truth.

There has always been a temptation in the life and worship of the church to appeal to the senses in a way that bypasses the mind, whether it be in the forms of worship the church employs, or the kind of disciplined life (or lack of it!) the church follows. It is very tempting to follow a course that makes people feel comfortable, excited, and happy, rather than that which promotes the sanctifying work of God in their lives.

It is hardly coincidental, therefore, that the consequence of this approach, as Peter sees it, will be that 'the way of truth will be blasphemed' (2:2). The ultimate casualty is the gospel itself. It is not merely that the church becomes a laughing stock in the eyes of the world, but God and his gospel are dishonoured. There is more truth than we care to think in the old English proverb that says, 'All that glitters is not gold!'

THEY ARE MANIPULATIVE

Given the fact that these false teachers clearly had a significant following and enjoyed great popularity, Peter does not mince his words. He says 'in their greed they will exploit you with false words' (2:3). Peter was not afraid to speak out against some of the most popular expressions of evangelical Christianity in his day. He clearly saw the dangers that were lurking behind the attractive exterior – dangers unseen by the crowds being drawn to it. When we strip off a few layers from the glossy image and the attractive ministries we soon discover what motivates and drives the false teacher – and it is not a pretty sight! 'Greed' is the mainspring of their ministry.

Financial gain has been one of the warped motivations for ministry since the day Simon the magician tried to buy a franchise in the apostolic ministry in Samaria (*Acts* 8:18–19). The desire for fame and influence has led others into the ministry to which God has not called them. Even though such teachers can be skilfully concealed, the spotlight of God's Word exposes them for what they are. It soon becomes evident whether such preachers are out to serve God or to fill their own pockets.

The other tell-tale sign that there is something not quite right about such ministries is that they will 'exploit' believers 'with false words'. In what sense can their words be said to be false? Only in that they diverge from the true words of Scripture. The best way to listen to sermons is with the pages of the Bible open before us. Only then, with our eyes fixed on the words of God and our ears open to the words of the preacher can we tell whether the preacher speaks according to the truth of Scripture.

Once again it may be tempting to step back from what Peter is saying and ask, 'Does it really matter? Aren't we in danger of becoming theological nit-pickers?' Actually, it does matter and it is the Lord Jesus who says so! It was Peter's Lord who warned his disciples of the many who would come in his name, but not with his message (*Luke* 21:8). The stakes are too high for us to be complacent about false teaching: it remains a 'clear and present danger'.

6

Those Who Play with Fire Get Burned

For if God did not spare angels when they sinned, but cast them into hell and committed them to chains of gloomy darkness to be kept until the judgment; ⁵if he did not spare the ancient world, but preserved Noah, a herald of righteousness, with seven others, when he brought a flood upon the world of the ungodly; ⁶if by turning the cities of Sodom and Gomorrah to ashes he condemned them to extinction, making them an example of what is going to happen to the ungodly; ⁷and if he rescued righteous Lot, greatly distressed by the sensual conduct of the wicked ⁸(for as that righteous man lived among them day after day, he was tormenting his righteous soul over their lawless deeds that he saw and heard); ⁹then the Lord knows how to rescue the godly from trials, and to keep the unrighteous under punishment until the day of judgment, ¹⁰and especially those who indulge in the lust of defiling passion and despise authority. Bold and wilful, they do not tremble as they blaspheme the glorious ones (2 Pet. 2:4–10).

It can be all too easy for us to play down the seriousness of doctrine that deviates from the truth – to be short-sighted when it comes to seeing the importance of truth in shaping the Christian life. Too often we hear it said, 'All that matters is the spreading of the gospel!' That may well be true, but what do we mean when we talk about 'the gospel'? The gospel is in fact much bigger than we often imagine it to be. When Paul, the great missionary-theologian, preached the gospel to the Ephesians, he preached what he later described as 'the whole counsel of God' (*Acts* 20:27). It is impossible to preach the gospel without reference to the whole of the Bible.

Some argue that the doctrine of God (in all its complexity) has nothing to do with the gospel; but the truth is that it has everything to do with the gospel. It is only when we realize that God is 'one' (*Deut.* 6:4) – that there are no other gods besides him, that he is Creator and Judge, but supremely that he is Saviour – that the gospel can make any sense at all. Or, again, someone might say, 'The doctrine of Scripture has nothing to do with the gospel.' But how can we take the message of the gospel seriously unless we know something about the character of the book in which it is found?

There are many doctrines that are vital to the gospel that are not found on the surface of its message, but which underpin its urgency and reliability. So here in these next few verses, Peter says more about false prophets and teachers, exposing the danger of following the message they bring. He spells out in no uncertain terms the destiny of such teachers and the consequences of their teaching for those who embrace it. Wrong beliefs lead to wrong behaviour, which in turn leads to judgment from God. The language Peter uses leaves us in no doubt as to what that entails: those who play with fire get burned.

However, we need to bear in mind that Peter is speaking primarily to fragile and weak Christians. His intention is not to terrify them, but to encourage them. Everything he says here by way of condemnation is interlaced with tender words of comfort. Does not that say something about the marks of a truly prophetic ministry? As it was for Jeremiah, so for all who are genuinely sent by God to minister his Word: they are not merely to 'uproot and tear down', but also 'to build and to plant' (*Jer.* 1:10, NIV). The word that rebukes is never divorced from the word that corrects and instructs in righteousness. With these things in mind, we can draw out three key elements from Peter's teaching in verses 4 to 10.

A WORD OF WARNING

In the opening verses of chapter 2 Peter has been speaking about the immediate effects of false teaching – its influence is destructive. Now he goes on to speak about the long-term and final consequences, both for those who propagate and for those who follow false teaching. The backdrop to this, at least in part, is the fact that Christians are often perplexed about the reasons why God allows such evil influences at all. This same sense of perplexity is seen in the parable of the weeds (*Matt.* 13:24–30, 36–43), in which the servants instinctively want to uproot the weeds from among the healthy plants before the time for harvest. The farmer's restraint on his servants, ordering them to wait until reaping time before separating the tares from the wheat, can be understood in the light of his care for the wheat. Damage could be done to the tender shoots of faith if immediate retribution fell upon spurious believers in their midst. It is better to wait for the final judgment when false professing Christians will be separated from true believers.

This is what Peter has in mind in this passage and he leaves his readers in no doubt as to what God will ultimately do with those who distort or deny his truth. He provides three clear examples from defining moments in God's past dealings with his enemies in Old Testament times and uses them as compelling reasons for every Christian to take this matter seriously.

The first example comes from the cosmic realm and concerns God's judgment on the rebel angels: these words of Peter may well refer to the rebellion of Lucifer, when he led a revolt in heaven and was cast out along with the angels who had followed him. Peter says, 'God did not spare angels when they sinned, but cast them into hell and committed them to chains of gloomy darkness to be kept until the judgment' (2:4). If these privileged and majestic creatures were not exempt or spared from such a judgment, how much less for those who enter into their revolt – even under the pretext of a gospel ministry.

The second example is drawn from God's dealings with the human race as a whole in the days of Noah (2:5). At that time, the judgment that was threatened was the very judgment that was finally enacted when Noah's contemporaries refused to heed the message he proclaimed. God makes no concessions, even when the majority of people are in opposition to him.

The third example comes from the destruction of Sodom and Gomorrah – an event that had already become a virtual synonym for judgment. Both cities had become engulfed in a life of unbounded hedonism with no thought of God and both were engulfed quite literally by fire (2:6). Their security and pleasure offered no protection from divine wrath.

It is not insignificant that Peter uses the same two metaphors of fire and water – the means of judgment in the days of Lot and Noah – to depict the final judgment of the world in the next chapter (3:6–7). God's warnings from the past have potent relevance to the future.

The bottom line in this strand of Peter's argument is that, considering what God has done in the past, he is well able to 'keep the unrighteous under punishment until the day of judgment' (2:9). What does that say to those who come in God's name, but not with his message, or to those who mindlessly follow them? It speaks a word of direst warning that none can afford to ignore.

A WORD OF PROMISE

Woven through these words of warning, as we have said already, are words of encouragement and promise. These are graphic reminders to us that the God of the Bible is indeed the God of wrath; but in wrath he remembers mercy (*Hab.* 3:2).

So, even when the entire human race was on the brink of divinely sent disaster, God raised up Noah and made him 'a preacher of righteousness' (2:5, NIV) – he offered the world salvation and deliverance *before* the flood! Whether he proclaimed God's righteousness by word, or deed, or both, is in one sense immaterial; what is clear is that he challenged multitudes around him for decades before the judgment came. Even within the most godless communities God has his 'preachers of righteousness': Christians who are prepared to stand up and speak out for him.

The same was true of Lot, described here as a righteous man (2:6). Despite the mess he made of his life and witness in Sodom, he still stood out as different from those around him. However feebly, he still tried to take a stand for God (*Gen.* 19:1–11). In one sense we can look at Lot and condemn him for his pathetic failures in the faith; but Peter shows that even in his weakness and failure, God was able to use him. What an encouragement that even the weakest Christians can function as 'salt and light' wherever God places them.

Again Peter presses home the logical conclusion of his argument: if this is so, 'then the Lord knows how to rescue the godly from trials' (2:9). From the examples he has used, it is clear that when God rescues his people 'from' such adversities, it is more often than not 'through' the adversity – preserving his people and bringing them safely out the other side.

Once more there is a double edge to what the apostle says here. Clearly he intends to comfort and strengthen Christians who are going through severe trials and hardships – perhaps through being on the receiving end of bitter persecution. He is reminding the suffering Christian that just as God has proved himself utterly reliable to those who trusted him in the past, so he will remain faithful to those who trust him in the present.

However, what he says also challenges and rebukes those who are tempted to look only to the present for fulfilment in life. To those who are creatures of circumstance, whose spiritual contentment varies according to what situation they happen to find themselves in, he gives the reminder that the Bible provides a much larger horizon for Christian living: namely, God's past revelation and his future promise. To focus merely on the present can be deceptive and serves only to undermine our faith; it actually mars our enjoyment of God in the here and now. We need to see God's bigger picture and be like Jesus, 'who for the joy that was set before him endured . . .' (*Heb.* 12:2)

A WORD OF INSTRUCTION

Peter's teaching in this section reaches a climax in its closing verses. The root of the problem he is addressing is found in what he calls 'the lust of defiling passions' which in turn he defines as a despising of authority (2:10).

What is the common denominator of all three examples of those who fell under God's judgment in the past? They all despised God's authority as it was and is revealed, not merely in his written Word, but in the structure and order of creation itself. There is a stark contrast between the essence of sin, which makes self the ultimate authority and reference point for life, and the essence of truth, which acknowledges the supremacy of God over both.

Because so much hangs upon it, how we understand and respond to his authority is absolutely crucial. A soccer star who has problems with the authority of the referee soon discovers who is really in charge of the game! The issue of disputed authority affects almost every sphere of life. In the home, the classroom, the community, and even the church – an aversion to authority can be seen – an aversion that stems ultimately from a rejection of the authority of God over the whole of life.

God's order and authority, once rejected, can only be replaced by one alternative: the authority of 'self', and that makes 'me' the centre of the universe. It is not surprising, therefore, that those who 'despise authority' are those who become embroiled in a life controlled by 'the lust of defiling passions'!

It is clear from what Peter says that this was (and remains today) a major issue in the life of the church. Whose authority is going to prevail? It is only when we recognize, acknowledge, and submit to the authority of God as it is revealed in Scripture and exercised through the various God-appointed structures in the church and the world, that we can discover God's true blessing. The anarchic spirit of sin is forever upending God's intended order for his world; it is only through his saving grace that the divine order can be restored (his kingdom established) and his people's lives re-ordered for his glory.

The warning of these verses is clear – Those who play with fire do get burned – but so too is the promise clear – Those who honour God will be kept safe and will be blessed eternally by him!

7

By Their Fruit You Will Know Them

Bold and wilful, they do not tremble as they blaspheme the glorious ones, ¹¹whereas angels, though greater in might and power, do not pronounce a blasphemous judgment against them before the Lord. ¹²But these, like irrational animals, creatures of instinct, born to be caught and destroyed, blaspheming about matters of which they are ignorant, will also be destroyed in their destruction, ¹³suffering wrong as the wage for their wrongdoing. They count it pleasure to revel in the daytime. They are blots and blemishes, revelling in their deceptions, while they feast with you. ¹⁴They have eyes full of adultery, insatiable for sin. They entice unsteady souls. They have hearts trained in greed. Accursed children! ¹⁵Forsaking the right way, they have gone astray. They have followed the way of Balaam, the son of Beor, who loved gain from wrongdoing, ¹⁶but was rebuked for his own transgression; a speechless donkey spoke with human voice and restrained the prophet's madness.

¹⁷These are waterless springs and mists driven by a storm. For them the gloom of utter darkness has been reserved. ¹⁸For, speaking loud boasts of folly, they entice by sensual passions of the flesh those who are barely escaping from those who live in error. ¹⁹They promise them freedom, but they themselves are slaves of corruption. For whatever overcomes a person, to that he is enslaved. ²⁰For if, after they have escaped the defilements of the world through the knowledge of our Lord and Saviour Jesus Christ, they are again entangled in them and overcome, the last state has become worse for them than the first. ²¹For it would have been better for them never to have known the way of righteousness than after knowing it to turn back from the holy

*commandment delivered to them. [22]What the true proverb says
has happened to them: "The dog returns to its own vomit, and
the sow, after washing herself, returns to wallow in the mire"*
(2 Pet. 2:10–22).

As every parent knows only too well, a major part of the child-rearing process is spent teaching children to recognize danger.
This takes time and effort because often those things that pose the
greatest threat to our children's safety are the ones that seem most
appealing to them.

This is precisely why such a large part of the Bible is devoted to
exposing the subtleties of false prophets and teachers – their power
lies in their appeal. So, a vital element in Christian maturity is the
ability to see beyond outward appearances and recognize the difference between what is true and what is false. Perhaps the most
familiar, yet most disturbing passage that deals with this matter is
found in the Sermon on the Mount. Jesus has many hard words to
say about false prophets: 'Watch out for false prophets. They come
to you in sheep's clothing, but inwardly they are ferocious wolves.
By their fruits you will recognize them . . .' (*Matt.* 7:15–20, NIV).
He not only condemns such people, but he also warns his followers
about how they should recognize them. The seriousness of this
issue can be seen in the large numbers of people who will be
deluded by their teaching and deprived of a place in heaven as a
result (*Matt.* 7:21–23).

As we listen to Peter developing the theme of the dangerous and
deluding influence of false teachers within the Christian church we
can hear echoes of Jesus' words to his disciples: 'By their fruit you
will know them.' In these verses Peter points to the kind of rotten
lives the false teachers lead. In exposing the truth about them in this
way, Peter is not being gratuitously judgmental, but is showing his
concern for the church and its welfare. As Michael Green says, 'Why
does he expend so much shot and powder on false teachers? –
Because he is a true pastor!'

How, then, are we to recognize such people and the kind
of influence they exert? – Peter identifies four things that stand
out.

THEY ARE BOLD AND ARROGANT

The ESV has put a paragraph break in the middle of verse 10 and rightly so. It highlights the visible traits that characterize the lives of such teachers, while at the same time holding on to their underlying cause. He has already told us at the beginning of this verse that these people 'despise authority', but how does this express itself publicly? By boldness and brashness in their attitudes and actions.

Peter says, 'Bold and wilful, they do not tremble as they blaspheme the glorious ones' (2:10). Their brashness is seen at its most audacious in the way they are not afraid to slander other people or beings of a higher rank and honour than themselves. It is not immediately obvious whom Peter has in mind when he speaks of 'the glorious ones'; but clearly his words point to the fact that the false teachers are blasé about authority. They show disdain for authority not merely in the different aspects of life on earth but almost certainly they think nothing of dismissing the power and authority of celestial beings.

Peter counters such behaviour by saying that even the angels of heaven would not dare to do anything like that – even when there might be just cause for doing so. He says by way of contrast, ' . . . whereas angels, though greater in might and power, do not pronounce a blasphemous judgment against them before the Lord' (2:11).

The point Peter is making is that even though it is right for Christians to judge in the sense of 'to be discerning', it is wrong to be of a condemnatory spirit. God alone has the prerogative to pass judgment on his creatures and their actions. That presents a sobering reminder to us that we need to be careful about what we say regarding other people and the attitudes we display towards them, whether to their faces or behind their backs.

Peter then focuses our attention on what causes false teachers to behave in this way: they are like 'irrational animals, creatures of instinct, born to be caught and destroyed' (2:12). The only 'authority' that governs their behaviour is that of their own animal urges, not the authority of God and the authority-structures he has built into his creation.

All this is very much an issue for a generation that elevates the authority of the individual above that of anyone or anything else. The curse of post-Enlightenment individualism has not only destroyed the structures and stability of society in general, but the authority structures of the church as well. Such arrogant self-centredness can never be the mark of a genuine child of God. A true Christian should be characterized by humility and a spirit of submission.

THEY LIVE FOR PLEASURE

It is hardly surprising that people whose lives are controlled by their instincts are also driven by a desire for pleasure. In particular, they are controlled by lust for sexual gratification and money.

That is precisely what bubbles to the surface in the behaviour of the false teachers whom Peter is describing. Indeed, their self-indulgence is so blatant that it becomes embarrassing: they are 'blots and blemishes, revelling in their deceptions, while they feast with you' (2:13).

Peter then points to Balaam as a graphic example of what such behaviour actually looks like and where it ultimately leads (2:15–16). Balaam was a prophet who sold his integrity for the riches offered by Balak, king of Moab. The king hired Balaam to pronounce a curse on the Israelites as they travelled through his territory (*Num.* 22:1–41). Balaam was driven by personal greed but was miraculously rebuked by the Lord through the mouth of his donkey! The point is sharp and cutting: even a brute beast could see that the prophet's life and ethics were warped. Those who are controlled by their urges and lusts are also blinded by them.

Peter warns the congregations to whom he was writing that false teachers not only harm churches, they actually harm themselves as well. Like the animals to which he has compared them, they are 'born to be caught and destroyed' (2:12). They will not get away with their sinful behaviour. Sooner or later their sinful lifestyles will catch up with them and they will be brought to a sudden end.

Two things flow out of what Peter says in this context. One is that pleasures – even the ones he has referred to here – though not wrong in themselves, must be kept within their God-ordained limits. We must look to God's Word to know how to discover their joy. The other is to realize how an appeal to sensual and emotional appetites can so easily be abused – especially in the life of the church.

THEY PROMISE WHAT THEY CANNOT DELIVER

The third identifying trait of the false teachers is disturbingly up-to-date in terms of popular Christianity. They make extravagant promises they cannot keep. One only has to look at the promotional material of many churches to realize why they are so appealing to the masses. Everything they do and offer is aimed at satisfying people's 'felt needs' – the hopes of the people are raised by extravagant and undeliverable promises.

The same was true in many of the churches of Peter's day which had come under the influence of the false teachers he condemns in this chapter. 'Speaking loud boasts of folly, they entice by sensual passions of the flesh those who are barely escaping from those who live in error. They promise them freedom, but they themselves are slaves of corruption. For whatever overcomes a person, to that he is enslaved' (2:18–19). They prey especially on recent converts, or Christians who are poorly taught, who inevitably are open and trusting towards those who claim to be Bible teachers. Anyone who sees such blatant exploitation will be repelled by it, and that is exactly how Peter responds. 'These are waterless springs and mists driven by a storm. For them the gloom of utter darkness has been reserved' (2:19).

The kind of preaching condemned here by the apostle can take many different forms: from the crass promises of health and wealth in some quarters to the more sophisticated allure of spiritual Nirvana in others. The surprising thing is not that so many people are taken in by this kind of message, but that so few people seem to be aware of its emptiness at the point of delivery.

THEY WANDER FROM THE WAY OF GOD

The closing verses of this chapter raise some awkward questions – not unlike other passages that deal with the sin of apostasy. Peter appears to be describing the false teachers as those who, at some point in their lives, have experienced salvation through Christ, but who lose it further down the line. Is it possible to be saved and then lost? Whatever the difficulties in trying to answer that question, one thing is clear: to all outward appearances apostasy and spiritual backsliding, for a time, look exactly the same. So the warnings attached to these verses ought to bring people in such a state to their senses.

The point that Peter has been emphasizing repeatedly is that the false teachers stray from the ways of God. Instead of going Christ's way like true disciples, they have become 'entangled' in the ways of the world (2:20). Although they 'have known the way of right-eousness', they 'turn back from the holy commandment delivered to them' (2:21).

From the beginning of the Bible to its end, God makes it clear that there are only two ways for us to follow through this life: his way and the way of the world – but only one leads to heaven. Jesus leaves us in no doubt about this when he says unequivocally, 'I am the way, the truth and the life. No one comes to the Father except through me' (*John* 14:6). It is not enough to pay lip service to Christ in claiming to be his followers; we need to demonstrate it by actually following where he leads.

The most distinctive thing about Christ's way is the cross. Far from being the way of self-pleasing and self-indulgence, it is the way of self-denial, suffering, and loss. 'If anyone would come after me', he says, 'let him deny himself and take up his cross and follow me' (*Mark* 8:34). Christians are not promised an easy passage through this world but rather the opposite: it is 'through many tribulations that we must enter the kingdom of God' (*Acts* 14:22).

The way mapped out by the false teachers is one that takes them right back to where they started. 'What the true proverb says has happened to them: "The dog returns to its own vomit, and the sow, after washing herself, returns to wallow in the mire"' (2:22). They end up being no different from the world!

It is a terrible thing to be conned – especially if it involves large sums of money. The person who has been deceived feels like kicking himself and regrets not having looked more closely at what was on offer. When it comes to spiritual deception, the issue could not be more terribly serious – not least because the consequences are eternal and irreversible. Peter is telling us that now is the time to check the credentials of those who make us great offers in the name of Christ. Now is the time to be sure that what they are offering to us is consistent with the Word of God.

8

Thinking Outside the Box

This is now the second letter that I am writing to you, beloved.
In both of them I am stirring up your sincere mind by way of
reminder, ²that you should remember the predictions of the holy
prophets and the commandment of the Lord and Saviour through
your apostles (2 Pet. 3:1–2).

It is the easiest thing in the world simply to 'go with the flow'.
Such an approach to life is straightforward and effortless. It is the
way the vast majority of people choose to live: they follow the trends
and fashions that prevail. Sadly, the same is true in many Christian
circles.

Things were little different in Peter's day – both in the secular
world and in the church – hence his reason for writing this letter
and hence his lengthy excursus addressing the problem of false
teachers in the previous chapter. Such people have an attraction and
popularity that is hard for others to resist. However, in this chapter
he returns to his central flow of thought and once again challenges
his Christian readers to learn to think differently. His whole aim is
summed up in the words: 'I am stirring up your sincere mind' (3:1);
or, as it is translated in the NIV, 'I have written . . . to stimulate you
to wholesome thinking'. He wants Christians to learn to use their
minds in the way God intended.

This is an issue of concern to people in all spheres of life – in
school, at work, and in the home; it is so tempting just to slip our
minds out of gear and coast through life, rather than think about our
actions and their motives. In the church, too, far too many Christians

do not think; not in the sense that they are unintelligent, but rather that they do not use their minds as they ought.

Why does the apostle make an issue of this? In his first letter, Peter highlights the importance of engaging our minds with the truth of God's Word. He says that we are to prepare our minds for action and to be sober-minded (*1 Pet.* 1:13). In other words, we cannot get to grips with what God is saying in the Bible without using our heads! But Peter also has more practical reasons for pressing this point. The way we use (or do not use) our minds will have a profound effect on how we understand the faith, how we worship, how we witness – it will affect our Christian experience in its entirety.

The link between these two reasons for clear godly thinking comes out powerfully in something Paul says at the climax of his message to the Romans. Having expounded the gospel in all its glory in the first eleven chapters, he begins to apply it in the twelfth with the words, 'Do not be conformed to this world, but be transformed by the renewal of your mind . . .' (*Rom.* 12:2). If we genuinely are God's children and really do belong to his family, then we are to buck the trends of this fallen world and conform to a very different life pattern – one that emerges from our experience of the grace of God in Christ.

The world that does not know God thinks in one way; the Christian, however, who knows God, thinks in a radically different way. The newborn Christian begins to 'think outside the box'. The implications of this are far-reaching in the extreme. To cultivating this new mindset three things are involved.

A MIND THAT IS NOT DISTRACTED BY THE SENSES

Right at the very heart of these two verses is a reminder of the reason why Peter is writing this letter in the first place. As we have noted already, it is in order to stir up in his readers what the ESV translates 'a sincere mind' or what the NIV more helpfully renders, 'wholesome thinking' (3:1). (We should probably note in passing that Peter's reference to this being his 'second letter' doesn't necessarily mean that the first he had in mind was actually 1 Peter; however, the debate over that issue can be better explored in the more technical commentaries.) What we are to be clear about is the fact that the whole purpose of this letter is Peter's desire for Christians to learn to think in a wholesome manner.

Michael Green in his commentary on 2 Peter picks up on the rather unusual turn of phrase in this expression and makes the observation that it was one of the favourite catch-phrases of Plato, the Greek philosopher. Plato used it to extol the virtues of what he perceived to be 'pure reason' – that is, 'reason uncontaminated by the seductive influence of the senses'. Whether or not this is precisely what Peter had in mind is a moot point; nevertheless, it ties in very neatly with the warnings of the previous chapter.

In those days, as we have noted, many Christians were being distracted by a kind of preaching that bypassed the mind and focused on the feelings. Its effect was to blunt the gospel and confuse people on the vital issue of what a Christian is.

Clearly this problem is not restricted to the first-century world Peter was addressing, but has an all-too-contemporary ring about it. The Anglican Bishop of Durham, Tom Wright, made this comment in relation to a moral debate that was having a damaging effect on his denomination:

> This debate is really about the role of reason. We don't do reasoned moral discourse any more. We do, 'I feel strongly about this', 'I feel wounded about that', and, 'Let me tell you about my pain' . . . We've slid into a post-modern morass which sounds like reasoned discourse but which is really just an exchange of strong emotions.

In an age in which learning and knowledge are more accessible than ever before, it is ironic that the ability to think clearly is in decline!

In speaking like this, Peter is not at all suggesting that Christians ought to have over-developed brains or that the gospel is only for academics. He may, in fact, be reflecting something of the pain and shame of his own past personal experience. Peter had once been a most impetuous person who was swayed more by his heart than his head. That led him into many sins and troubles. So his concern here is to show that a right understanding of God, the gospel, and our-selves must take precedence over everything else. Nowhere is such a concern expressed more clearly than in the words of Jesus: 'You will know the truth and the truth will set you free' (*John* 8.32)!

A MIND THAT IS NOT DULLED THROUGH FORGETFULNESS

Peter seems to be gripped with the need to give his readers repeated reminders – they are emblazoned across the opening chapter (1:12–15). Now here, as he picks up the threads of his argument, he says he is stirring up their mind 'by way of reminder' (3:1) and he does so in order that they 'should remember' (3:2). Why must he take such pains to press this point? Because Christians are so prone to forget things they need to remember for the good of their souls!

It was a major problem for God's people in the Old Testament (*Isa.* 17:10), for the disciples during Jesus' earthly ministry (*Mark* 8:18), and for Christians in the New Testament churches (*Gal.* 1:6; *Heb.* 5:12). It is not merely that it is all too easy to forget what the gospel actually teaches (as was the case with the Galatians), but we can so easily lose sight of how the gospel is to shape our lives. We forget the link between what we believe and how we are to behave.

The first recipients of this letter were falling at both hurdles. The teachers who misled them peddled a distorted view of the Christian life, and that led to a distorted understanding of the gospel. It is frightening to see the consequences of forgetfulness in life generally, but even more so to see the consequences of a forgetful spirit among Christians.

Several things flow by way of application from this. One is to realise that this is actually a problem that affects us all. No Christian and no generation of Christians can presume that they know it all, and always have what they need to know at their fingertips. We need to take to heart the words in Arabella Hankey's well-known hymn, 'Tell me the old, old story': 'Tell me the story often, for I forget so soon!' We can never know the gospel too well or too personally.

The second note of application is the need for us to take positive steps to remedy the problem of our forgetfulness by all the God-given means at our disposal – the so-called 'means of grace'. The ministry of the Word, the blessings of baptism and the Lord's Supper, the privilege of prayer, and the joy of Christian fellowship are all ways in which the truths lying at the very centre of the Christian life can actually be kept at the centre of our daily experience.

Perhaps most of all, as we reflect on Peter's teaching, we will realise that we can never live and labour in the way God desires unless we first understand, not merely the 'how to' of the Christian life, but primarily, the 'how can?' The essence of the Christian life is rooted in Christ – all that he is and has done for us – and we can never truly live that life without conscious reference to him at every point along the way.

Once again we find ourselves being steered back to the words of Jesus, this time in his great high priestly prayer. He not only makes it clear that the truth and nothing but the truth can liberate us in this world but that the truth, and nothing but the truth, can truly change us. He prays, 'Sanctify them in the truth, your Word is truth' (*John* 17:17). This sanctifying life transformation can only come about through our regular exposure to the truth of God.

A MIND THAT IS NOT DIVERTED FROM THE SCRIPTURES

Once more – even in such a relatively short letter – Peter repeats himself. He does so to draw attention once more to the centrality of Scripture in the Christian life. All he is saying is so that his readers 'should remember the predictions of the holy prophets and the commandment of the Lord and Saviour through your apostles' (3:2).

These have both been mentioned earlier in his letter. The reference to the predictions of the holy prophets points us back to what he has said about the holy Scriptures (1:19–21) and the reference to the commandment of the Lord, to the gospel in all its fullness (2:21). This repetition is called for because of the way the false teachers were diverting the attention of the Christians away from the Bible – partly by focusing on the emotional and the sensual, partly by offering alternative forms of revelation. Peter is determined to restore his readers' focus on God's written Word.

In turning the people's attention away from God's Word to their own feelings and desires, the tactic of the false teachers was really no different from that of Satan in the Garden of Eden. His approach to Eve threw doubt on God's revelation: 'Did God actually say . . . ?' (*Gen.* 3:1), and, 'You will not surely die. For God knows that when you eat of it [the tree] your eyes will be opened and you will be like God, knowing good and evil' (*Gen.* 3:4–5).

It was William Tyndale who first used the adjective 'evangelical' to describe Christians who were Word-centred and whose lives were primarily shaped by the Bible. He did so by way of reaction against the mediaeval mysticism of his day and the kind of Christianity that focused more on religious rituals and drama than on the lifechanging message of Scripture. Pre-Reformation religion bore little resemblance to the Christianity found in the Bible.

Jesus taught his disciples that the truth will liberate and transform them only when his words – the words of Scripture – abide in their hearts (*John* 15:7).

A mere glance around most major Christian bookstores will reveal the kind of books that are today's bestsellers. Many of them are either of the 'How to' variety, or else proclaim a message of extraordinary experience. If such books mark the trends in modern Christian reading, then huge questions are raised about what tomorrow's Christianity will look like. Peter's call to the church of his day needs to be heard and heeded by the church in our own. We need to learn afresh how to think 'outside the box' – not merely of a secular world, but also of a Christian world that has lost its biblical moorings.

9

So, They Think God Has Forgotten?

*Knowing this first of all, that scoffers will come in the last days
with scoffing, following their own sinful desires. ⁴They will say,
'Where is the promise of his coming? For ever since the fathers
fell asleep, all things are continuing as they were from the
beginning of creation.' ⁵For they deliberately overlook this fact,
that the heavens existed long ago, and the earth was formed out
of water and through water by the word of God, ⁶and that by
means of these the world that then existed was deluged with water
and perished. ⁷But by the same word the heavens and earth that
now exist are stored up for fire, being kept until the day of
judgment and destruction of the ungodly.*

*⁸But do not overlook this one fact, beloved, that with the Lord
one day is as a thousand years, and a thousand years as one day.
⁹The Lord is not slow to fulfil his promise as some count slowness,
but is patient toward you, not wishing that any should perish,
but that all should reach repentance. ¹⁰But the day of the Lord
will come like a thief, and then the heavens will pass away with
a roar, and the heavenly bodies will be burned up and dissolved,
and the earth and the works that are done on it will be exposed?*
(2 Pet. 3:3–10).

There has been no shortage of ridicule aimed at the Bible's
teaching on the return of Christ. In drama, literature, and
music we meet with parodies and jibes that mock the idea that the
Jesus who walked this earth two thousand years ago will somehow
return as described in the Bible. But, then again, that mockery is as
old as Scripture itself and was something Peter was familiar with
during the early days of the Christian church.

The promise of a glorious, public, and personal return was a major strand in the teaching of Jesus. His followers had firmly grasped it, but only after the traumatic events of his death, resurrection, and ascension, and many of them were anticipating an early fulfilment of his promise, possibly within their own lifetime. However, at the time Peter wrote, there was still no sign of its taking place. This 'delay' raised questions in the minds of genuine Christians and prompted ridicule from the opponents of the gospel. The church found itself struggling on two fronts!

These issues that surround our Lord's return rumble on in much the same way right down to the present day. It is not just that there is a wide range of views within the Christian community as to what Jesus meant in his teaching concerning his return, but there is relentless scepticism about the whole subject in the minds of those who are outside the church.

How, then, should Christians respond? Peter answers that question by telling us not to be surprised by the presence and the attitude of scoffers. Such scoffers will come in the last days and they will pour scorn on the teaching that Jesus will return (3:3–4). Do not be taken unawares and do not be shaken by it. God's saving plan has not been blown off course now, any more than it had been when Israel waited for the first appearance of the Messiah.

Peter then lists four things that supply a response to those who pour scorn on this strand of Christ's teaching and that provide an anchor for the faith of those who patiently wait for it.

GOD'S WORD

Those who scoff at the idea of a personal and visible return of Christ base their thoughts on what they observe in creation. 'They will say, "Where is the promise of his coming? For ever since the fathers fell asleep, all things are continuing as they were from the beginning of creation."' (3:4). They think that the visible, tangible realm is the final arbiter in what can be known or can happen.

The same notion has been the most popular basis for rejecting, not just what the Bible says about the end of the age, but about the supernatural in general. People instinctively feel secure in the realm of the material world they think they know so well. But Peter argues that there is something more, which lies behind what is seen, which we need to factor into our reckoning. The problem with the scoffers' approach is that it requires even more faith on their part than the approach of those they choose to ridicule. When we try to make sense of the life, history, and destiny of this world without reference to the God of the Bible, we are left with even bigger unanswered questions. For those who believe in a self-originating world and universe, the unanswerable question is, 'How did matter come into existence in the first place?' Those who try to explain the order and harmony that are the hallmark of the cosmos need to answer the question, 'How do you account for design without a Designer?'

Peter says about such people, 'For they deliberately overlook this fact, that the heavens existed long ago, and the earth was formed out of water and through water by the word of God, and that by means of these the world that then existed was deluged with water and perished. But by the same word the heavens and earth that now exist are stored up for fire, being kept until the day of judgment and destruction of the ungodly' (3:5–7). It is not merely that they 'overlook' certain important facts, but that they do so 'deliberately'.

What is it they overlook? Two defining moments in history: the creation of the world and the judgment of the human race in the flood. Peter points out that, in both cases, events did not take place of their own accord, or by natural causes, but both were a direct consequence of God's powerful Word. Even though 'water' was the agent involved in both cases, the Word of God was the instigating cause behind them.

Because that is true of what happened so dramatically in the past, so Peter reasons, we can believe it to be true of what is prophesied in the future (3:7). We have no reason to doubt that the same Word that was powerful and true in the past will be powerful and true in the future.

Here, then, is the first big issue with which we need to wrestle. How are we to make sense of the world and all that has happened, is happening, and will yet happen in it? By means of the Word of God, which God has not only given, but has also authenticated down through the ages. God has chosen to reveal himself in a way that demonstrates a constant interface between his spoken/written Word and the events of world history. This is uniquely true of the 1,500-year period during which the Bible was given. God's words and deeds were so inextricably interwoven that failure or falsehood in the one would expose failure or falsehood in the other. God deliberately put his reputation on the line in a way that was open to scrutiny. Had he, or those who spoke in his name, been lying, it would have been immediately apparent.

Nowhere is this more obvious than in the way that Jesus so publicly predicted, not just his death by crucifixion, but also his resurrection. He might well have been able and willing to orchestrate the former, but he certainly could not orchestrate the latter, if he was merely a man! His entire integrity was bound up in the link between his words and their fulfilment.

The same Word that enables us to make sense of the past, allows us to make sense of the future too.

GOD'S TIMETABLE

The second strand in Peter's response to the scoffers is his critique of their view of time. They demand, 'Where is the promise of his coming? For ever since the fathers fell asleep, all things are continuing as they were from the beginning of creation' (3:4). They look at time purely from a human point of view. They reason that if certain things have continued for a long time, then they must surely hold true for all time. Peter immediately takes them into God's very different perspective. He does so by means of the Word of God to which he has already alluded.

He quotes from a Psalm that is all about God and his relationship to time, where it says, 'For a thousand years in your [God's] sight are but as yesterday when it is past, or as a watch in the night' (*Psa.* 90:4; cf. 3:8). That statement simply makes the point that time looks very different depending on the vantage point from which it is viewed: God's or man's.

How many times, while on a long car journey, have parents heard their children ask, 'Are we there yet?' A child's perception of time is very different from an adult's; how much more then is our perception of time bound to differ from that of the eternal God? Peter is actually taunting these mockers and insinuating that there is really something quite childish in their argument; they have made themselves, not God, the reference point from which to measure time.

This reminds us that God's timetable and ours are not the same. That is true not merely in the grand scheme of history, but also in the 'little scheme of things' as God's plan unfolds in our personal lives. What patience and trust the Old Testament saints were called to exercise in the vast sweep of time between God's initial promise of a Saviour (*Gen.* 3:15) and its fulfilment with the incarnation of Christ. No doubt there were scoffers during that intervening period too! Likewise, appreciating the scope of God's timetable will help us to exercise patience and trust in our present circumstances.

GOD'S PURPOSE

As Peter's line of reasoning unfolds, we discover that far from casting aspersions on the character of God, the delay in Christ's return actually displays more of his grace and glory. Peter argues, 'The Lord is not slow to fulfil his promise as some count slowness, but is patient toward you, not wishing that any should perish, but that all should reach repentance' (3:9). This is one of those verses which, at first sight, seem perplexing, but which, on closer inspection, actually are not. The ESV captures the meaning well. Peter is not merely saying that God is delaying this event to show he is patient with the world generally, but he is speaking of God's patience with believers particularly. It is 'with you' – his people – that he is showing patience.

This puts a double edge on what Peter is saying. On the one hand, Christ's return is delayed until 'every one' of 'you' comes to repentance and faith. That is, until the full number of those whom God has planned to save is actually saved. None of God's chosen ones will be lost.

On the other hand, the return of Christ is also delayed so that 'you' – God's people – may fulfil the responsibility of taking the gospel out to the whole world. The gospel is the means by which God fulfils his purpose in election and it is the church's duty to preach the gospel to all nations so that the 'elect from every nation' are brought to saving faith in Christ. People are not saved in a vacuum, but through the preaching of the gospel.

We can apply Peter's teaching in two ways. The first is that since God does not waver in his purpose, his children should not falter in their faith – regardless of what the scoffers may say. The second is that if God has planned the salvation of those he has chosen from before the beginning of time, and if he has ordained the fulfilment of that plan through the preaching of the gospel, then it falls to us to proclaim that message in obedience to his commission.

GOD'S JUDGMENT

Peter's final argument in response to the scoffers is a warning: the very thing they ridicule and reject is the thing that will ultimately take place, and bring with it their everlasting ruin.

He warns them that the day of Christ's return will come 'like a thief' (3:10) – at the very moment when it is least expected. When will that be? When it is too late to do anything about it! The repeated plea of New Testament (and Old Testament) writers is to ensure we are ready now – before it is too late.

That day will also have consequences for the whole universe: 'The heavens will pass away with a roar, and the heavenly bodies will be burned up and dissolved, and the earth and the works that are done on it will be exposed' (3:10). This will be no localized judgment, but one that will touch the outer limits of all God has made. Just as high-profile judicial investigations are instructed to 'leave no stone unturned', so it will be with the ultimate act of justice in this world. Since no part of creation was left untouched by man's fall and its consequences, so no part of creation is beyond the need for the purifying and restoring work of Christ.

So the day will come with devastating consequences: everything will be laid bare under the scrutiny of God's all-seeing eye. Nothing that has been concealed will remain concealed. Everything will be brought to light.

The gentle irony of it all is that the very fact that Peter is sounding this note and issuing this warning is not evidence of vindictiveness on his part, but of compassion. He warns his readers in order that those who need to hear his warning might take his message to heart. It is only when we understand that we must finally face God as the Judge of all the earth and give an account to him, that we realize we are not prepared for the day of judgment to dawn. Only by looking to the Christ who has already faced the judgment of God on behalf of sinners like ourselves, can we be delivered from the wrath to come (*1 Thess.* 1:10). It is impossible to contemplate these things without being forced to ask the question, 'Am I ready?'

10

The Difference a Day Makes

Since all these things are thus to be dissolved, what sort of people ought you to be in lives of holiness and godliness, [12]waiting for and hastening the coming of the day of God, because of which the heavens will be set on fire and dissolved, and the heavenly bodies will melt as they burn! [13]But according to his promise we are waiting for new heavens and a new earth in which righteousness dwells.

[14]Therefore, beloved, since you are waiting for these, be diligent to be found by him without spot or blemish, and at peace. [15]And count the patience of our Lord as salvation, just as our beloved brother Paul also wrote to you according to the wisdom given him, [16]as he does in all his letters when he speaks in them of these matters. There are some things in them that are hard to understand, which the ignorant and unstable twist to their own destruction, as they do the other Scriptures (2 Pet. 3:11–16).

'What a difference a day makes!' – so sang Dinah Washington. A day can make a world of difference to our lives – whether it comes on us unexpectedly or is one that we have anticipated and for which we have prepared.

Nowhere is that more true than with regard to that one day that will end all others – that is the day Peter has in mind in these verses. It will not only make a world of a difference to our present life; it will make an eternal difference to our final destiny. It is a day that looms large on the horizons not only of New Testament teaching, but also of the entire message of the Bible, as God's purpose for the world and for the human race is there mapped out.

The prospect and consequences of the day of judgment are given such a high profile in Scripture in order that we might learn to think about our life in this present world in a different light. Even cold statistics tell us that the average person tends to think more about the present than he does about the future. The fact that few people have much by way of savings and make precious little provision for their retirement says it all. People today live by the age-old philosophy: 'Eat, drink, and be merry, for tomorrow we die!'

This tendency is all the more serious when we factor into it a spiritual dimension. The problem with the 'tomorrow we die' approach to life is that death is not the end. There is a vast eternity that stretches out beyond this present life and we need to be ready for it. The Preacher in Ecclesiastes reminds us that everyone, deep down, is aware of this fact because God 'has put eternity into man's heart' (*Eccles.* 3:11). But even though everyone has this awareness of eternity, relatively few take it seriously and live in the light of it. However, in many and various ways we are continually being reminded that neither we, nor the world we live in, will go on forever. How will you respond to the inevitable?

Peter addresses this very question in this next section of his letter. He directs our attention to the day that will stand out from all others and urges us to think about it and all its sobering implications. Seriously contemplating the future will affect us in at least three ways.

THE WAY WE VIEW THE FUTURE

We have said already that what dominates this passage is its distinctive view of the future – a view that is grounded, not in human speculation, but in divine revelation. It pivots on what Peter strikingly describes as 'the day of God' (3:12) – an unusual expression, but one that picks up certain Old Testament expectations. It will be the day on which God will be seen to reign supreme. The God who is there, but who has been so largely ignored, defied, and rejected by this fallen world will finally be seen and acknowledged as God the Lord.

There are two sides to what this truth means in practice. The first has been mentioned already (3:10), but is repeated here (3:12): this will be a day of cosmic judgment which will affect the entire created order. It will not just affect the human race but the entire creation. Just as creation was contaminated by the consequences of human sin, so it will be purged and purified by God's supreme act of judgment.

All this reminds us that our rebellion has consequences for the world and universe of which we are a part. Just as human recklessness and greed lie behind the countless ecological disasters affecting the planet and even the growing pollution of space itself, so too in a more sinister way the sin that is bound up with that recklessness and greed touches the outer reaches of the universe in ways we cannot fully fathom. The disorder sin has brought into our lives has had the knock-on effect of bringing disorder into creation itself.

It is not hard to see what Peter has in mind here and why he says that such drastic action will be necessary on God's part when the day of judgment dawns. When a landlord comes to repossess a property that has been leased to unscrupulous tenants, he has a major clean-up operation on his hands to restore it to its original condition. The same will be true when our tenancy in our God-given home expires. God has not abandoned his good intentions for a world that he made well and pronounced 'very good' (*Gen.* 1:31), even though we, his tenants, have spoiled it.

Peter not only sounds this negative note about what the 'day of God' will mean, he flags up its wonderful positive implications too. Yes, we are to anticipate that day with dread and trembling, because it will mark the end of the world as we know it; but at the same time we can look forward to this day which will see the 'new heavens and a new earth' ushered in (3:13). They will be 'new' in the sense of having an altogether different quality from anything we have known in this present world – they will be characterized by 'righteousness'. They will be 'the home of righteousness' (NIV), in the sense that righteousness will no longer be a temporary visitor to a creation violated by sin. The new heavens and earth will be the permanent abode of righteousness.

As Peter sets out the monumental truths that attach to this coming day of the Lord, he wants us to stop and ask ourselves, 'How do we view the future?' Are we like the proverbial ostrich that sticks its head in the sand – content with the world as we know it – a world that is second best and that will not last? Or are we looking forward to something infinitely better?

The way we view the future has enormous implications, not only for the way we view the present, but for what we do with the opportunities it offers.

HOW WE FACE THE PRESENT

When a student has an important exam scheduled for a particular date, the way he or she spends the days, weeks, and even months leading up to it will be seriously affected. A scheduled future event can have a massive impact on the present. So it is with the future event of the return of Christ – in line with the entire New Testament teaching on this subject (*Matt.* 24:42–44; *1 John* 2:28). Peter spells out the practical implications that flow directly from the prospect of the future as God has revealed it to us (3:11).

'Since everything will be destroyed in this way, what kind of people ought you to be?' (3:11, NIV). His question to his readers is as straightforward as the answer he supplies: 'You ought to live holy and godly lives . . . ' (3:11, NIV). The logic of Peter's reasoning is this: if the future world is one in which righteousness reigns and which is suffused with God's presence, now is the time to start getting ready for it.

The problem with many people is that they say on the one hand, 'When we die we want to go to heaven', but when asked if they really want God and his righteousness in their lives here on earth, they give an altogether different response! The same can be strangely true for some Christians. They say they are looking forward to spending eternity with God in heaven, but find it hard to 'endure' one hour per week in his presence on earth.

Peter presses home his point more powerfully and painfully by saying, 'Therefore, beloved, since you are waiting for these, be diligent to be found by him without spot or blemish, and at peace' (3:14). Here is another practical implication that emerges from the prospect of 'the day of God'. Once again there is a double edge to it: we are to ensure that we are reconciled to God, not rejected by him; and that we are in harmony, not at odds with him.

This amounts to nothing less than a call to radical discipleship. It calls for 'diligence' or concentrated effort. As we prepare to meet God on the day of Christ's return, we will make the knowledge of God the focus of our entire existence. Only when we are certain of our standing with him (1:10) can we live lives that will not only honour him, but will also enjoy his fullest blessing, in this world and the next.

WHERE WE PLACE OUR CONFIDENCE

The big question that hangs over everything in these verses is this: 'What is the basis of this view of the future?' There is no shortage of wild and wacky ideas about the future on offer today, but what warrant do we have to believe any of them?

Even in the first-century Roman world of Peter's day, theories about the future abounded – many of them literally etched on tombstones that have since been discovered or excavated. Some saw no future and so advocated a life of hedonism in the present: 'I was nothing then, I am nothing now; so, you who still live, eat, drink and be merry, for tomorrow you die.' Others likewise, who did not believe in an after-life, embraced a spirit of apathy in this life: 'Once I had no existence, now I have none. I am not aware of it, it does not concern me.' Yet others peered into the future beyond this world and saw only despair: 'Charidas, what below? – Deep darkness. But what of paths upwards? – There are none. Then we are lost!' Every human instinct leads us to fear that there is nothing positive for us to anticipate when we leave this world behind. If, then, we are to have a genuinely optimistic outlook on the future, we need good, solid reasons for it. This is precisely what Peter provides in the remaining verses of this section.

The roots of this Christian hope of Christ's return and the blessings to follow – what Paul describes as 'our blessed hope' (*Titus* 2:13) – lie entirely in what God has revealed of himself and his redemptive purpose in his written Word. Peter wants his readers to know that what he is advocating in this letter is not some novel idea or teaching, but that which God has disclosed in Scripture from the beginning.

The hope of the 'new heavens and a new earth' is entirely consistent with 'his promise' (3:13) – the promise that was first made known through the prophet Isaiah (*Isa.* 65:17). In other words, the expectation of this great and as yet unfulfilled event in the future is bound up with that great corpus of Old Testament expectation already fulfilled in the coming of Christ. Peter is arguing that if God's Word in the Old Testament has demonstrated itself to be true to such a large extent already, then there is no reason to doubt the fulfilment of every detail in the future.

This should encourage his Christian readers to be patient as they await the fulfilment of the promise. 'And', he adds, 'count the patience of our Lord as salvation, just as our beloved brother Paul also wrote to you according to the wisdom given him, as he does in all his letters when he speaks in them of these matters. There are some things in them that are hard to understand, which the ignorant and unstable twist to their own destruction, as they do the other Scriptures' (3:15–16).

The word 'salvation' here is used in the sense of the full outworking of God's planned and purchased redemption, not just in the individual's experience, but also in its worldwide application. This grand theme has been the burden of the writings of the New Testament apostles, just as it was with their Old Testament predecessors, the prophets. God has spoken through them and what they have written is 'Scripture' – the very words of God.

To express himself in this way – putting the apostolic writings on the same level as the Old Testament Scriptures – was a very bold and daring thing for a New Testament author to do; but that is precisely what Peter does here. The New Testament authors were deeply conscious that they were not speaking their own words, but that God was communicating his own words through them. They expected their hearers to recognize the Word of God and respond accordingly (*1 Thess.* 2:13). In making such a claim, they were also inviting the same scrutiny of the New Testament writings as was applied to the Old, so that 'all Scripture' (*2 Tim.* 3:15–16) might prove to be worthy of our trust for salvation. Nowhere could that be more significant than with respect to how to view the future, and how to frame our lives in the present.

Peter's words could hardly be more pertinent. What better way, then, to end our comments on this passage than to ask the very same question he did? Since you know these things to be true – because God himself has made them known to you – what kind of person ought you to be?

11

Keeping Both Feet Firmly on the Ground

You therefore, beloved, knowing this beforehand, take care that
you are not carried away with the error of lawless people and
lose your own stability. ¹⁸But grow in the grace and knowledge
of our Lord and Saviour Jesus Christ. To him be the glory both
now and to the day of eternity. Amen (2 Pet. 3:17–18).

The final verses of this letter bring us, not merely to the
conclusion of what Peter has to say, but to the glorious climax
of his message. Here is the pinnacle of his teaching and application.
Here is the heart and soul of his letter to his brothers and sisters in
Christ, who were in danger of being destabilized in their faith, not
so much through external pressures from the world as through
pressures from within the church. Here is what they need to know
to keep both feet firmly on the ground.

We cannot but feel that a note of personal testimony lies behind
these closing exhortations. It is as though the apostle sees something
of himself in the believers to whom he is writing. There had been a
time in his own Christian experience when he had been both eager
and immature. Like so many Christians today Peter was full of
spiritual zeal, but lacking in depth and stability.

Peter had learned the hard way that one of his greatest needs was
simply to grow up spiritually. He discovered through his own
personal failure – when he denied his Master three times – just how
shallow and fickle his heart really was. It was through the risen
Christ's gracious dealings with him (*John* 21:15–19), that he began
to realize where true spiritual experience is to be found: in rich and
deep communion with Jesus. Painful though this experience was for
Peter, it marked a turning point in his life and ministry. The Peter

we see in the Acts of the Apostles and in his Letters is so different from the Peter we meet in the Gospels. Yet, ironically, it was only because he had made progress in the faith by this painful route that Peter was now able to empathize with and minister to those who shared his past weaknesses.

So here in these closing lines of his letter, he issues one final exhortation to his readers to press on in the faith towards the goal of spiritual stability and maturity, and outlines how this can be accomplished.

BEING ON GUARD AGAINST LAWLESS MEN

Everything Peter says, though blunt and pointed, is bathed in love and affection for his readers. He addresses them as 'Beloved' (3:17), 'My dear friends'. Such love provides the context for the challenging and heart-searching things he has been saying. It is only when there is a bond of true Christian love that there can be effective instruction in the faith – the kind of robust engagement that will challenge personal weakness and encourage spiritual growth.

As he addresses his readers in this way, Peter candidly tells them that there is really nothing new in what he has been saying to them. They had heard beforehand the things he had written in his letter. It had been part of the systematic teaching they as Christians had received. This reminds us once more that the answer to our deepest needs in the Christian life is not to be found in new spiritual revelations or experiences, but in a clearer understanding and appreciation of what we have already been taught, and the application of these glorious truths to our daily living. What we do with what we have learned is really at the heart of spiritual maturity. As one wise Christian once said, 'It's not the things I don't understand that give me problems; it's the things I do understand!' Peter's readers were being tempted by the false teachers to think there was some kind of deeper knowledge or mysterious experience that they needed – something that they as yet did not know or understand.

Peter's concluding words throw down a final challenge to the false teachers who were unsettling the church. Since what his Christian readers needed most was a firmer grasp of what they had been taught from the beginning, Peter says to them, 'Take care that you are not carried away with the error of lawless people and lose your own stability' (3:17). Again, he was in a very real sense drawing on his own sad experience. It was because he had not listened to Jesus' words and warnings and because he had not given heed to Jesus' exhortation to 'watch and pray' that he crumbled when the pressures came. So here he urges his readers not to fall into the same trap.

How were they to exercise such vigilance? By being alert to the influence of what he calls 'lawless people'. These are the people whom he has described at some length as false teachers and scoffers (2:1–3; 3:3–4). They were a threat because they were unwilling to submit to the Word of God. Their bad example encouraged others to walk in the same lawless ways.

Vigilance is needed because the presence of lawless people within the church is not always patently obvious. It must also be said that lawless people have not always been unconverted people! In some cases they have been Christians who have not been willing to yield to the rule of God's Word. Such are, quite literally, law-less – they are a law unto themselves. If we appreciate what Peter is saying here, we will not only be alert to the influence of those around us, but we will take heed to the influences at work in our own hearts. We will realize that vigilance must begin with ourselves and with our own hearts, because that is where the seeds of rebellion against God take root.

Here, then, is the first of Peter's final exhortations and it is a negative one: if we are going to stand firm in the faith, we must first of all be on our guard against the spirit of lawlessness in ourselves and in those around us.

ALWAYS GROWING IN KNOWLEDGE AND LOVE

The second of Peter's closing exhortations could hardly be more positive: 'But grow in the grace and knowledge of our Lord and Saviour Jesus Christ' (3:16). The verb form Peter uses here is a present active imperative. In other words, it is not some kind of one-off experience he has in mind, but a steady growth that continues throughout the whole of the Christian life.

It is sobering to note how many major deviations from the Christian faith have come in on the back of a widespread longing for some kind of spiritual panacea. This longing is not unlike the childish mentality of a ten-year-old who wishes he was fifteen, or a fifteen-year-old who wishes he was twenty! Just as there is no magic formula or growth hormone that can produce instant maturity, so there is no spiritual cure-all that can bring about instantaneous fulfilment in the Christian life.

Instead, spiritual fulfilment is found through the *grace* and *knowledge* of the Lord Jesus Christ. Both of these ingredients for growth are disarmingly simple, yet incredibly profound. (This is true of all the essentials of a healthy life!)

Growth comes through the '*grace*' of our Lord and Saviour Jesus Christ. Grace is first and foremost God's unmerited favour – hence its priority over knowledge. We can only know Christ because God has graciously made him known to us and graciously given us the ability to know him for ourselves. It is not because of any natural ability in us or because we somehow deserve it but entirely of God's free kindness and love.

The roots of our Christian experience lie in the fact that God accepts us, not because of who we are or what we have done, but because of who he is and all that he has done for us through his Son. When we get that principle fixed in our minds and hearts, it provides the cornerstone for stability in our Christian living. Our acceptance with God is found through Christ, not ourselves. The Bible also uses 'grace' to mean divine energy or power. When the writer of Hebrews speaks of 'grace to help in time of need' (*Heb.* 4:16) he is referring to the supernatural strength God provides for his children to enable them to face life's every contingency. So here, as Peter speaks about our ongoing need to 'grow in grace' he has in mind our need to draw increasingly on those divine reserves of strength which God has freely put at our disposal through his Son by the inner workings of his Holy Spirit in our lives. We not only need to appreciate where we find our acceptance with God, we also need to depend on him now: in both cases through Christ alone.

The Bible also uses 'grace' to mean godlike character. When John says that Jesus was 'full of grace and truth' (*John* 1:14) he is pointing as much to his godlike character as to the way he dealt with sinful people. There was a graciousness about Jesus that was a perfect reflection of the graciousness of God, because Jesus the man was nothing less than God in human flesh. So, as Peter urges us to grow in our relationship with Christ he is saying that we must grow to be more like him. To be Christlike is to be godlike, or truly godly.

Having said this, Peter makes it clear again that such growth in grace can never be separated from 'the *knowledge* of our Lord and Saviour Jesus Christ'. Our Christian character and experience grow out of our knowledge of Christ. It is not just that we need to have an increasingly clear and accurate understanding of who he is and all that he has done, but also that this must lead us more and more into a deeper personal relationship with him. Having been brought into union with him through faith, we need to grow in our communion with him in a living and dynamic relationship. The union established between a man and a woman on their wedding day must be nurtured and deepened during the whole of their life together. The same is true in a Christian's spiritual marriage to Christ. A relationship exists, but as with all relationships, it needs to grow and mature.

The beauty of our relationship with Christ is that there is always more to learn about him and always scope for further growth and enrichment in our fellowship with him. Therein lies the second ingredient in what Peter has to say about progressing towards maturity and stability: we need to cultivate an ever-deepening relationship with Christ.

BEING GIVEN OVER TO THE GLORY OF CHRIST

The final ingredient is unlike the others in that it does not come in the form of an exhortation, but rather a doxology. It is seen in the climactic explosion of praise and adoration that marks the end of his letter: 'To him be the glory both now and to the day of eternity!'

This is a remarkable expression, not least because of what it says about Jesus. This is one of the highest ascriptions of praise given to Christ anywhere in the New Testament. Such high praise was normally reserved exclusively for God; so for Peter to ascribe it to Jesus Christ is to make the boldest of assertions that Jesus *is* God. But it stands to reason that this assertion is true, for every aspect of the Christian life and what we need to live it, as set out by Peter, must be obtained from God alone. So for him to point his readers repeatedly to Christ for these spiritual resources as he does is in fact to point them to God.

Once more we cannot but see something of Peter himself behind this great statement. Here was the disciple who, when he was with Jesus during his earthly ministry, appeared to be fully committed to him, but in reality was fully committed to himself. Now, as an older man with years of Christian experience behind him, he pens these words, and it is quite possible that his tears mingle with the ink. It is only when Christ is given the pre-eminence and glory he alone deserves that all things begin to fit properly into place in every way. He alone has power to save his people and rescue the world he has made. He alone has the authority and ability to re-order all things by his wise and loving rule. He alone is able to do all this because he is God. Within the unimpressive confines of his human flesh are the limitless resources of God himself. That is why he is uniquely worthy of our praise and adoration.

So, given the dimensions of his great salvation, all praise and glory belongs to him, not just for the 'now' of this present age, but till the 'day of eternity' – that day which will usher in the everlasting 'day', or age, of eternity. It is an unusual expression, but one that is clearly linked to 'the day of God' (3:12).

What, then, is Peter's message to Christians still living in the 'now' of God's timetable? Quite simply that we must decrease so that Christ may increase! And what is his message to those who are not yet Christians, who live in this present age? That now is the time and opportunity for getting ready for that future day and all it will usher in. Now is the time to prepare for eternity because when 'the day of eternity' dawns it will be too late and there will be no second chances.

In many ways Peter has brought us full circle as he draws his letter to a close. He began with prayer for abundant grace to be given to his Christian readers through 'the knowledge of God and of Jesus our Lord' (1:2). He has stated from the outset that 'all that pertains to life and godliness' has been fully and freely provided in what God has accomplished and made known through his Son (1:3).

It is fitting, therefore, that he should conclude his letter by proclaiming the glory of Christ, and urging his people to know and trust him more!

THE LETTER OF

JUDE

I

Contending for the Faith

Jude, a servant of Jesus Christ and brother of James,

To those who are called, beloved in God the Father and kept for Jesus Christ:

²May mercy, peace, and love be multiplied to you.

³Beloved, although I was very eager to write to you about our common salvation, I found it necessary to write appealing to you to contend for the faith that was once for all delivered to the saints. ⁴For certain people have crept in unnoticed who long ago were designated for this condemnation, ungodly people, who pervert the grace of our God into sensuality and deny our only Master and Lord, Jesus Christ (Jude 1–4).

Have you ever stumbled across a long-lost letter somewhere and wondered who wrote it and why was it written? Even if we do not recognize the signature at the end of the letter, there is something in us all that makes us curious about the times, circumstances, and context in which it was written.

The same is true with this little letter, tucked away almost at the end of the New Testament. The fact that it does not bear the name of one of the more prominent figures of the New Testament only makes us wonder all the more about its author and his reasons for writing.

Some of these questions have been covered already in the introduction to this volume under 'Authors and Dates'. Jude, whose name
appears as the first word in this letter in its original form, is probably
none other than the half-brother of Jesus, who is mentioned in
Matthew's Gospel (*Matt.* 13:55). But we must dig a little deeper to
find out more about Jude.

The fact he identifies himself as 'a servant of Jesus Christ and
brother of James' (verse 1) says several things about him. It tells us
something about how Jude understood himself. He could have
reminded his readers of his close family ties with Jesus – that would
have given his brief letter a considerable amount of weight in the eyes
of some of his readers – 'Jude, the half-brother of Jesus'. Instead,
however, he calls himself 'a servant of Jesus'. As Jude grew up with
Jesus there may have been a time in his life when he viewed his older
brother with the kind of familiarity that concealed a measure of
contempt (cf. *John* 7:1–5). He had, however, reached a point in his
life when he realized that Jesus was more than just his half-brother;
Jesus was his Saviour and Lord. Now he is not ashamed to describe
himself as 'a servant of Jesus Christ'. Now that Jude was 'born again'
Jesus was his true elder brother!

Jude's self-description also says something about the concern he
had for the churches to which he was writing. There was no shortage
of correspondence circulating among the New Testament churches
at that time and much of it was used as a vehicle for men to make a
name for themselves under the pretext of pastoral concern. Not so with
Jude. He may not have been a high-profile figure in the church, but
he was the servant of a high-profile Master whose concern for the
church was infinitely greater than anyone else's. Jude writes at his
Lord's behest and communicates the message his Lord had given him.

His focus in the letter is clearly not on himself, but on his fellow
Christians who were finding themselves in troubled waters. From
the very outset, he wants to impress on them a number of things that
are crucial for their spiritual well being.

REMEMBER WHO YOU ARE

The first lesson comes out in the way Jude describes the recipients
of his letter. He addresses them as 'those who are called, beloved in

God the Father and kept for Jesus Christ' (verse 1). Straight away he is reminding these beleaguered Christians of who they are.

Trouble and adversity have their own way of undermining our self-esteem and confidence in life – and that can be true of Christians too. We only have to think of Job in the Old Testament and some of the terrible things he says about himself in the midst of his suffering to see how his whole sense of dignity and worth was almost destroyed. In times of trouble, the only antidote is to turn one's gaze away from self and circumstances to what one is in fellowship with God through Christ. Three things come into view from what Jude writes.

The first is that Christians have been *called*. Jude actually uses a word here that is in the past tense, but that carries with it a sense of ongoing significance. Something happened to these people in their past that has abiding implications for their present: God had called them through the gospel.

Jude has something more in mind than what is sometimes described as the general call of the gospel – what Jesus refers to when he says, 'Many are called, but few are chosen' (*Matt.* 22:14). There is a sense in which the call of the gospel goes out to all who hear it; but not everyone who hears this general call responds to it as they ought. However, Jude is thinking about the special call of God by which the Father, through the Holy Spirit, uses the summons of the gospel to capture the hearts of the hearers and draw them to himself. He fills the words of the gospel with a spiritual magnetism that cannot be finally resisted. Even though we are by nature hostile to God and unwilling to submit to him, he by his grace overcomes this hostility and makes the unwilling willing in a way that often surprises us.

The wonderful thing about this effectual call which brings us into fellowship with God through faith in Jesus Christ is that it resonates in our ears all the way through our Christian experience. Hence the nuance given in the translation we are using. It is the call to discipleship – to be followers of Jesus (*Mark* 1:16–20). The voice of Jesus which called the first disciples to become his followers was the same voice that led them on, even after his ascension. Supremely it is the call of Christ that keeps us going heavenward in our earthly Christian pilgrimage. In Paul's words, 'I press on towards the goal for the prize of the upward call of God in Christ Jesus' (*Phil.* 3:14). Above the clamour of the hostile voices in the world around them, the voice of Jesus still echoed in the ears of these first-century believers, just as it does for all true believers in every age.

Jude also addresses his audience as those who are *'beloved in God the Father'*. It is not only young children who respond to the troubles of life by crying, 'Nobody loves me!' Too often adults can feel the same self-pitying emotions. Perhaps these early Christians felt bereft of love on account of the troubles and problems confronting them. If so, Jude here reminds them of the love that really matters. Whatever the insecurities of their earthly relationships, they were held firm in the one relationship that transcends them all: they were 'beloved in God the Father'. God loved them. Few themes have given more inspiration to Christian hymn-writers over the years. The words of George Matheson capture well the comfort Jude was seeking to impart to his readers:

> O Love that wilt not let me go,
> I rest my weary soul in Thee;
> I give Thee back the life I owe,
> That in Thine ocean depths its flow
> May richer, fuller be.

In addition to being *called* and *loved*, those to whom Jude wrote could take comfort in being *'kept for Jesus Christ'*. Some translations have opted for 'by' or, 'in Jesus Christ', probably because such renderings seem more natural and certainly fit in with wider New Testament teaching. But the ESV translation is the most accurate rendering of what Jude actually wrote. He wants to remind his Christian hearers that (as Matheson's hymn says) our lives are no longer our own. Because God in his love has redeemed us – bought our freedom through the blood of his dear Son – we belong to him and therefore, we are his. As Paul says, 'You are not your own, for you were bought with a price' (*1 Cor.* 6:19). This is true, not only for all Christians individually, but for the church corporately. As the bride of Christ the people of God are being kept and prepared for the day when the heavenly Bridegroom will come to take her to his home!

Because these things are true on the God-ward side of this relationship, certain other things are guaranteed on the church-ward side. Jude has every warrant for saying, 'May mercy, peace and love be multiplied to you' (verse 2). Everything we need and our soul deeply longs for – 'mercy, peace and love' – come to us through our living, vital relationship with God through his Son.

When we go through hard times in life we all tend to panic. But the first sensible response to such a state of panic is to sit down and remind ourselves of those things that are absolutely true and on which we can utterly rely. This is how Jude begins this letter addressed to the embattled Christians of his day – *remember who you are!*

STAND UP FOR WHAT YOU HAVE

As Jude launches into the main body of his short letter, he begins with what seems like an apology. He says, 'Beloved, although I was very eager to write to you about our common salvation, I found it necessary to write appealing to you to contend for the faith that was once for all delivered to the saints' (verse 3). It appears that his original desire had been to write about the glory of the gospel – the 'common salvation' that bound him to them, and them to him, and all of them together to God. But circumstances demanded that his focus be placed elsewhere. Instead of indulging in the luxury of savouring the gospel, he feels it necessary to call God's people to the defence of the gospel for reasons that will become clear in the verses that follow.

That said, it would be wrong to think that in issuing this 'call to arms' he has totally abandoned his deeper longing to revel in the greatness of God's salvation. As we work our way through this letter and see his thoughts unfold, we shall notice that the very thing which the church is called upon to uphold and defend is what actually upholds and defends the church! The survival of the gospel does not depend on the strength and defensive powers of the church, but *vice versa*.

It is important that we understand what Jude means when he talks about 'the faith that was once for all delivered to the saints'. Even though there is an argument for seeing it as 'faith' in the sense of the experience of faith – our enjoyment of salvation – that view does not sit neatly with what he goes on to say. His concern is for the defence of a body of truth which was being undermined and threatened by false doctrine.

It makes more sense, therefore, to understand 'the faith' as referring to the body of truth that comprises the gospel – those great truths of divine word and deed on which the gospel rests. Elsewhere in the New Testament this body of truth is referred to as 'the standard of teaching to which you were committed' (*Rom.* 6:17), 'the pattern of sound words you have heard from me [Paul]' (*2 Tim.* 1:13) and 'the good deposit' entrusted to our care (*2 Tim.* 1:14), to name but three.

Jude, however, is not simply talking about the written revelation of God that we have in the Bible (though that is certainly in view); but, instead, the teachings that emerge from that revelation – the doctrines contained in the Bible. That is why the apostles drew a distinction between teaching that was sound or healthy and that which was not. The church is called to make sense of the message of Scripture and spell out the component parts of the gospel. Some strands of its teaching are 'of first importance' (*1 Cor.* 15:3) and essential to the gospel and a true experience of salvation. By inference, therefore, other parts of its message are of secondary importance and leave room for different interpretations without harming the shared experience of salvation among God's people. Here Jude is concerned about the core doctrines of the Christian message. These must be defended at all costs because salvation itself depends upon them.

The word translated '*contend*' is a strong word and says a great deal about the degree of effort and even pain that is involved in this spiritual struggle to which every believer is called. On the one hand, it alerts us to the energy and commitment called for on our part. 'Stand up, stand up for Jesus!' is the battle cry of the church. We cannot afford to be soft and careless when it comes to defending the faith.

On the other hand, it reminds us, that 'we do not wrestle against flesh and blood, but against the rulers, against the authorities, against the spiritual forces of evil in the heavenly places' (*Eph.* 6:12). Behind the human face of the opponents of the faith is the dark complexion of Satan himself. Our fight cannot be waged in human strength alone; we need the strength that God supplies through Jesus Christ.

The fact that the word Jude uses here is from the Greek word that gives us our English word 'agony' indicates that for some at least, this battle will be very costly. Martyrs have shed their blood for the sake of the gospel, and continue to do so in many parts of the world today.

Too often we fail to appreciate the gospel and the wonderful salvation it provides. It is only when we grasp the greatness of God's salvation that we will realize the importance of contending *'for the faith once for all delivered to the saints'*.

BEWARE OF THOSE WHO UNDERMINE

Jude justifies his decision to switch from glorying in the gospel to urging his readers to contend for it, by pointing to events that were taking place in the churches at the time of writing: 'For certain people have crept in unnoticed who long ago were designated for this condemnation, ungodly people, who pervert the grace of our God into sensuality and deny our only Master and Lord, Jesus Christ' (verse 4).

Clearly the people Jude has in mind pose a subtle threat to the church because of the way they have 'crept in unnoticed'. Great damage can be done to the church from within its own ranks by those who may at first sight seem more than plausible in their faith and life. Jesus warns his disciples about the 'leaven of the Pharisees' (*Mark* 8:15). Leaven was like yeast: small in size, but incredibly powerful in its influence. Elsewhere he warns, 'Beware of false prophets, who come to you in sheep's clothing but inwardly are ravenous wolves' (*Matt.* 7:15). While Jesus' words are not an excuse for paranoia, they nevertheless are intended to put us on our guard. Christ himself puts us on notice that such people will always be around. The devil delights to masquerade as an angel of light (*2 Cor.* 11:14) and we should not be surprised if he turns up in that guise among those whom Jesus describes as 'the light of the world'!

Two aspects of these 'ungodly people' are exposed that show not only how warped their teaching is, but also how warped they are in themselves. They 'pervert the grace of God into sensuality' and they 'deny our only Master and Lord, Jesus Christ'. They turn the concept of grace into a licence to sin, not unlike those who were perverting the gospel of grace, whose false doctrine Paul addresses in his letter to the Romans (*Rom.* 6:1–4). In the gospel, grace and law are not mutually exclusive, but rather inseparably joined; but always in that order – grace first, then law following on. We see it in the Ten Commandments. Before God gives the Law to his people (*Exod.* 20:3–17), he first reminds them that he is their gracious Saviour. It is because he saves through grace that he expects his saved people to walk in the way of his commandments.

However, it is not merely this awful slur on God's grace that is of deep concern to Jude. He also resents the aspersions the false teachers are casting on 'our only Master and Lord, Jesus Christ'. The One who is the very embodiment of grace and law, and through whom alone God saves and blesses, is demeaned and denied by their false gospel. It is little wonder that Jude puts the church on a war footing against such evil people.

Indeed, he says that these false teachers were 'long ago designated for this condemnation'. These words are not easy to interpret. Some take them to mean that the condemnation that will fall upon these people was foretold from earliest times in the Bible. Others understand Jude to be referring to God's purpose in predestination. Just as Judas' actions and fate were bound up with God's eternal plan and purpose (*Acts* 2.23), so too are the actions and fate of the false prophets in view here. It may well be that we do not need to choose between these two alternatives because actually both are true. The false prophets are not outside God's eternal purpose – they cannot derail the good he has planned – and we are not left in ignorance about them. The Bible is full of warnings alerting us to these people and why we must be wary of them.

So, Jude's opening words set the scene. It may well have been with a degree of relief that his first readers received his letter because the situation that had been confusing and troubling them was now beginning to make sense. Much as Christians in every age would love the life of faith to be straightforward and stress free, this is rarely if ever the case. To answer Christ's call in the gospel is to enlist in his army and to stand beneath his banner!

2

Warnings from the Past

Now I want to remind you, although you once fully knew it, that Jesus, who saved a people out of the land of Egypt, afterward destroyed those who did not believe. ⁶And the angels who did not stay within their own position of authority, but left their proper dwelling, he has kept in eternal chains under gloomy darkness until the judgment of the great day – ⁷just as Sodom and Gomorrah and the surrounding cities, which likewise indulged in sexual immorality and pursued unnatural desire, serve as an example by undergoing a punishment of eternal fire (Jude 5–7).

History is full of warnings and we ignore them at our peril. Human nature is such that the terrible things that man has done to his fellow man in the past have a sinister habit of recurring in the present under a different guise, but with the same effect. When we think of genocide, we tend to think of names like Hitler and Stalin and the mass murders for which they were responsible; but there have been countless other genocides since their day, several of which have taken place outside the glare of international scrutiny. History brings home some painful truths about our human condition.

The same is true in terms of our race's spiritual history and, perhaps especially, the history of the church. There is a significant element of repetition in the way things have gone wrong in the life of the church. It is not just that God's people fall into the same sins and failures generation after generation – though that is true – they also fall foul of the same kinds of false teaching and are led away from God down well-trodden paths.

As Jude sets out to press home the seriousness of what was facing the church in his day, he begins by pointing to the past. It is clear from the way he says things in this letter that he has a fondness for groups of three, and here he gives three historical examples of rebellion against God and the consequences that followed. The examples quoted have not been chosen at random. Each one has links with the issues raised by the presence of the false teachers in the church. Although the form of their rebellion may have differed, the underlying causes were the same, and so too were the consequences, in terms of the divine response.

This emphasizes the timelessness of Jude's message. He helps us to identify the roots of spiritual rebellion in the human heart – roots that are to be found in every human being, even Christians – and he warns us about their dangers. He begins by saying, 'I want to remind you' of these things (verse 5). By saying this he is not implying that they are suffering from memory loss; he is calling them to a solemn biblical duty. Throughout the Scriptures, many reminders and exhortations to remember certain things are issued for the purpose of ensuring that truth controls our actions. When we read that 'God remembered his covenant with Abraham, with Isaac, and with Jacob' (*Exod.* 2:24), there is not the slightest suggestion that God had suffered from amnesia; rather it teaches us that his covenant was consciously controlling his actions.

This comes out forcibly in the way Jude frames his words here. He issues this 'reminder' – ' . . . although you once fully knew it'. These things had not slipped from their memories, but they had slipped from their place as the controlling factor in their lives. These sobering truths from Bible history, though known by Jude's readers, were no longer tempering their relationship to God with reverence and awe and influencing their behaviour for good as they faced the temptations common to the people of God in all ages.

We will look in turn at the three examples given by Jude, along with their salutary lessons for the present.

THE ISRAELITES AND THEIR UNBELIEF
The first thing Jude reminds his readers of is 'that Jesus, who saved a people out of the land of Egypt, afterwards destroyed those who

did not believe' (verse 5). Some other versions use the designation 'Lord' instead of 'Jesus' – a difference that reflects a variation in the manuscripts on which the text of the New Testament is based. The majority of manuscripts use the title 'Lord', but some of the oldest surviving manuscripts have 'Jesus'.

As with many such differences, having to choose between the alternatives does not pose a major problem, nor does it create difficulties over the reliability of the text. The central confession of the New Testament is 'Jesus is Lord' (*Rom.* 10.9). Both titles refer to the same person. However, if (as seems highly plausible) the ESV's decision to opt for the earlier reading is correct, Jude is making a very striking statement about Jesus and his role in Old Testament redemption.

There are other passages that refer directly to Old Testament believers and their understanding of God's promise of a Messiah. Jesus told his Jewish opponents, 'Your father Abraham rejoiced that he would see my day. He saw it and was glad' (*John* 8:56). The writer of Hebrews said of Moses, 'He considered the reproach of Christ greater wealth than the treasures of Egypt' (*Heb.* 11.26). Even though Jesus was not physically present in the Old Testament (apart from his pre-incarnate appearances, called *theophanies*) he was present spiritually, and, by faith, the Old Testament saints were made aware of this truth.

The impact of this for Jude's New Testament readers is to reinforce the weight of the illustrations he cites. The same Lord Jesus who revealed himself through these sobering events of the Old Testament is the One to whom they are accountable. They and we should be under no illusions about Jesus. He is not only 'Gentle Jesus, meek and mild', born of Mary, come to save; he is also the Judge before whom we all must one day stand and give an account.

What does Jude say about Jesus and what he did during the Exodus? We are told that he not only 'saved a people out of the land of Egypt', but that he also 'destroyed those who did not believe'. This was a well-known fact about what happened in the wilderness during the forty years between the Israelites' leaving Egypt and taking possession of the Promised Land. What we need to be clear about, however, is his use of the language of salvation. The Bible clearly uses the Exodus as the most important Old Testament act of deliverance on God's part. It was used as the symbol of salvation in the fullest sense of the word. However, that did not mean that all who were part of the great company that left Egypt were true believers and had experienced salvation in the sense of deliverance from sin and its eternal consequences. In fact, the majority did not actually trust in God and repeatedly grumbled and rebelled against him. They were the ones that Jesus destroyed. Only their children and a few others were allowed to enter Canaan.

Jude's purpose in citing this Old Testament example is to highlight the reason for the destruction of these people: they were destroyed on account of their unbelief. Even though they had seen God's mighty acts, heard his voice, and experienced his blessing, they still refused to trust him fully and so brought upon themselves the consequences of their unbelief. It was a salient reminder to those who professed to be Christians in New Testament times that it is possible to be part of the visible church of Jesus Christ without actually being one of his people. The same has been true in all ages. The evidence of our truly being part of the church as the body of Christ is having a living faith – that we live by trusting in the promises of God and walking in his ways. Supremely this means trusting in that greatest of all the promises – that salvation is to be found through Jesus Christ, God's Son.

REBEL ANGELS AND THEIR REJECTION OF AUTHORITY

In the next verse the scene shifts from what happened in the desert to what happened in heaven. Jude now speaks about 'the angels who did not stay within their own position of authority, but left their proper dwelling' and what happened to them (verse 6). Their sin was that of rejecting God's authority by abandoning the position he had given them.

Angels are not figments of our imagination, or mythical figures in folklore, but are real beings, according to the Bible. They have been created by God and given specific roles and responsibilities in his wider creation. The writer of Hebrews calls them 'ministering spirits sent out to serve for the sake of those who are to inherit salvation' (*Heb.* 1:14). Jesus says they are spiritual creatures who are different from human beings in that they neither marry nor are given in marriage (*Matt* 22:30). Nevertheless, they are accountable to God and are expected to acknowledge his authority.

Jude speaks about an angelic revolt against God's authority. He does not specify where and when it took place – he may have had a single event in mind, or he may have been thinking of a succession of events. The point is that they rebelled against divine authority and were now suffering the consequences of their sin.

These rebellious angels were now being 'kept in eternal chains under gloomy darkness until the judgment of the great day'. Jude is referring to what theologians have often called 'the intermediate state'. Human beings experience this between physical death and the general resurrection of the dead at the return of Christ. It is a state of conscious existence, involving two separate places and conditions for the spirits of believers and unbelievers who have departed this life (*Luke* 16:19–31).

For the fallen angels, it is a kind of spiritual remand centre where they are held along with those human beings who have rejected God on earth. In 'eternal chains' and under this 'gloomy darkness' they await the day of judgment.

Once more the warning is clear and plain to all. God has spoken frankly about these matters and put them on record in his Word for all to read and heed. If even the very angels of heaven are accountable to God, then so are those who profess to be God's people on earth, but who refuse to submit to his authority.

Jude's words of warning have far-reaching implications for the anti-authoritarian spirit that pervades our secular world and, sadly, so much of today's church as well.

SODOM AND GOMORRAH AND THEIR SEXUAL LICENCE

Jude's last citation in the trio of examples he gives is of Sodom and Gomorrah – two cities whose names have become a byword for sexual perversion. They were a hotbed of the worst kinds of vice and even the description given of what went on within them (*Gen.* 19:4–8) is so explicit (certainly in the Hebrew) that it is difficult to read it without feeling a sense of disgust.

Jude leaves us in no doubt about what the people of these infamous cities were charged with and why they suffered divine punishment: they 'likewise indulged in sexual immorality and pursued unnatural desires' (verse 7). (Jude's use of 'likewise' to preface this third comment is clearly linking the sin of these cities with that of the rebel angels and may point to the unusual incident involving the 'sons of God' and the 'daughters of men' recorded in Genesis 6:1–4.) Whatever the link, the message is clear: sexual licence brings God's judgment where there is no repentance.

Jude has already drawn attention to the fact that the false teachers who were doing so much damage in the church were doing so by their lifestyle as well as by their teaching. They lived a life of 'sensuality' (verse 4). Down through the ages there have been all kinds of attempts to accommodate sexual deviance within the church. From the cover-ups of adultery and child abuse to the open acceptance of homosexual practices, the church has mimicked the world rather than courageously lived by the sexual ethics of her Creator. While it may be true that the church and some of her teachers have at times been prudish about expounding the Bible's teaching on this subject and left her people with a distorted view of sex, the Bible is clear in what it has to say on this subject. Sex is not only for procreation, but is also God's good gift to man and woman that enriches and blesses their relationship in marriage.

Even though we belong to a generation that has sinned against God by abusing this good gift of his, the beauty of the gospel is that Christ is able and willing to forgive those who have fallen into the same kind of sins of which Sodom and Gomorrah were guilty. A shining example of the grace of God is seen in the experience of the Christians in Corinth. Some of them had been prostitutes, homosexuals, and others had even been involved in incest before Christ had saved them. It is important for us to remember the grace of Christ: he is still 'the Friend of sinners'. Christ's people are to accept those rescued from immoral lifestyles, just as God has accepted them in Christ.

Jude has no difficulty in accepting this aspect of the gospel of grace. However, his concern in these verses relates to those who claim to believe this gospel, but who effectively deny both the gospel and the Saviour of whom it speaks by bringing sexual immorality into the church.

The warnings Jude issues in these verses may be drawn from the distant past, but they have a chillingly contemporary ring to them. The very things that brought divine displeasure and judgment in former ages are all too evident today. They are the kinds of things that invite the criticism and condemnation of Christ in his letters to the churches in Revelation (*Rev.* 2:1–3:22). We would be naïve in the extreme to think that today's church is immune from such teaching and behaviour, or that we are somehow exempt from its consequences. Here is a history lesson that should make us sit up and think!

3

A Warning about Spiritual Conmen

Yet in like manner these people also, relying on their dreams, defile the flesh, reject authority, and blaspheme the glorious ones. [9]But when the archangel Michael, contending with the devil, was disputing about the body of Moses, he did not presume to pronounce a blasphemous judgment, but said, 'The Lord rebuke you.' [10]But these people blaspheme all that they do not understand, and they are destroyed by all that they, like unreasoning animals, understand instinctively. [11]Woe to them! For they walked in the way of Cain and abandoned themselves for the sake of gain to Balaam's error and perished in Korah's rebellion. [12]These are blemishes on your love feasts, as they feast with you without fear, looking after themselves; waterless clouds, swept along by winds; fruitless trees in late autumn, twice dead, uprooted; [13]wild waves of the sea, casting up the foam of their own shame; wandering stars, for whom the gloom of utter darkness has been reserved forever.

[14]It was also about these that Enoch, the seventh from Adam, prophesied, saying, 'Behold, the Lord came with ten thousands of his holy ones, [15]to execute judgment on all and to convict all the ungodly of all their deeds of ungodliness that they have committed in such an ungodly way, and of all the harsh things that ungodly sinners have spoken against him.' [16]These are grumblers, malcontents, following their own sinful desires; they are loud-mouthed boasters, showing favouritism to gain advantage (Jude 8–16).

We are used to seeing 'Wanted!' posters and warning messages issued by the police to alert the general public to the presence of dangerous criminals in the community. The most insidious criminals are conmen who pretend to hold some respectable position – safety inspectors, government officials, or the like. They may possess seemingly impressive credentials, but in reality they are thieves who want to gain access to the homes of vulnerable people. Warnings need to be given about such people, who are extremely skilful in the art of deception.

Jude does much the same thing in these verses as he elaborates on what he said already about the false teachers and their influence in the churches to whom he was writing. He has warned his readers about the threat these men pose, and spoken of the judgment that awaits, not only them, but all those who follow them. He has reinforced this warning with three graphic lessons from history – spelling out the particular sins that surfaced in each case and the divine punishment that followed. He now goes on to expose these false teachers in all their hideous colours.

Some who read this section of Jude's short letter are troubled by it because two of its main arguments are drawn from non-biblical writings, which seem to be quoted as though they were authoritative documents. One seems to be drawn from an ancient book known as *The Assumption of Moses* (a book to which Origen, one of the early church fathers, refers) and the other is a quotation from *1 Enoch*. Both would have been well known in Jude's day. They belonged to a collection of Jewish writings known as the *Pseudepigrapha* – spiritual writings penned by Jews under the pseudonyms of well-known figures from the Bible, but not recognized, even by the Jews, as belonging to the canon of Holy Scripture.

It is not hard to see why such quotations are disturbing to Christian readers, not least because other parts of the *Pseudepigrapha* and a similar body of ancient literature – *The Apocrypha* – have given rise to certain heretical teachings, such as the doctrine of Purgatory. However, if we look closely, not only at what Jude quotes, but also at the way in which he quotes, we realize that he is blending these references with other allusions to well-known passages from the Old Testament. It seems that, like Paul when he quoted the Greek poet Epimenides while addressing the Areopagus in Athens (*Acts* 17:28), Jude is simply using literary references familiar to his readers as illustrations of biblical truth.

As we listen to what he has to say, three very clear warnings emerge. These alert us, on the one hand, to *the evil characteristics of these people, and how we are to recognize them*, and on the other hand, to *their utter folly*. As with their secular counterparts, spiritual conmen are dangerous precisely because of their appealing plausibility. Therefore, Christians beware!

THEIR AUTHORITY AND IGNORANCE

Jude makes a direct connection between what he has said already about the Israelites, the fallen angels, and the cities of Sodom and Gomorrah, and 'these people' who behave 'in like manner' (verse 8). Just like their Old Testament counterparts, these false teachers should arouse suspicion on account of the authority to which they appeal in order to justify their teaching and conduct.

They rely on 'their dreams' and use them as the pretext for rejecting authority (most notably that of the Bible), and even for blaspheming 'the glorious ones' (verse 8). (The term 'Glorious ones' is used here in the sense of 'angelic beings', as we can deduce from the example given in the following verse.) Jude wants to highlight the fact these men were dreamers. He is not merely saying that they were living in a dream world of their own delusions, but something more subtle. He uses a word that elsewhere in the Bible refers to prophetic revelation. During the entire period when God was revealing his Word, alongside the true prophets and genuine dream-revelation, there were false prophets and those whose dreams were not from God (*Jer.* 23:16). Likewise, in the early church there were true prophets whose message came with God's authority; but there were also false prophets whose authority was merely their own. The test of the authenticity of any particular prophecy or purported revelation from God was whether it was consistent with the rest of God's revelation in Scripture (*Isa.* 8:20).

The message of the false teachers whom Jude condemns failed the test. They used their teaching to justify defiling their flesh, rejecting authority, and blaspheming angels. Jude counters their bad example by alluding to the good example of the archangel Michael, as he disputed with the devil over the body of Moses (verse 9). As we have said already, Jude's choice of example is fraught with difficulties, because he seems to oppose the unbiblical authority of the false prophets by an appeal to an extra-biblical document! Richard Bauckham in the *Word Biblical Commentary* on Jude offers the most straightforward explanation of this: 'The point of contrast is that Michael could not reject the devil's accusation on his own authority.' Even if the example was taken from tradition rather than Scripture, it was a tradition that upheld a scriptural truth and principle.

We may find it difficult to understand Jude in the example he chooses, but he is crystal clear in his application of it to the false prophets: 'But these people blaspheme all that they do not understand, and they are destroyed by all that they, like unreasoning animals, understand instinctively' (verse 10). Their spurious authority is rooted in their brute-like ignorance. Just as animals live by instinct and appetite rather than by reasoned response to authority, the same is true for these people. Their understanding is not shaped by the true and safe authority of God's Word, but by the warped instincts of their own fallen human nature.

Jude immediately follows this with a description of the kind of people who were wreaking havoc among the first-century Christians. We might add that their successors have done the same among Christians throughout the world down the centuries since. The fallen human instinct of a preacher appeals strongly to the same fallen human instinct in his (or her!) hearers. When this is presented as a message from God, it becomes all the easier for the hearers to respond to it. (It always sounds so much more spiritual when false teaching is prefaced by the words: 'God has told me . . . ') But lest we should be duped, Jude warns us to stop and examine the credibility of the teacher. Is this teacher really speaking from God?

THEIR MOTIVES AND INFLUENCE

The pleasant smile and the smooth demeanour of doorstep conmen form a thin veneer that hides a sinister motivation. It also conceals from view the pain and loss such people leave behind them. The same is true of the fatal attraction of the false teachers and their perverse message. Jude pronounces a 'Woe!' upon these false spiritual guides and rolls out another triplet of examples to enforce his point (verse

11). He points to Cain, Balaam, and Korah, who all illustrate the kind of twisted motives that can govern people's behaviour and the farreaching consequences of their sinful behaviour.

Cain made a name for himself as the world's first murderer (*Gen.* 4:1–12). 'The way of Cain' seems to be an allusion to the motives that prompted him to take his righteous brother's life. The apostle John sheds further light on Cain's motives: 'We should not be like Cain, who was of the evil one and murdered his brother. And why did he murder him? Because his own deeds were evil and his brother's righteous' (*1 John* 3:12). Cain was motivated by envy which led on to murder. Envy is an insidious reality. It is not restricted to coveting another person's material prosperity; we can so easily be envious of another person's spiritual gifts and influence. Paul speaks of preachers he knew who preached Christ 'from envy and rivalry' (*Phil.* 1:15)! Ministerial envy, leading to rivalry, is a common and destructive influence within the Christian community. Jude peels back the façade of these false teachers and shows us the ugliness of what lies beneath.

He also compares them to Balaam, the prophet from Moab whose heart was motivated by the love of money (*Deut.* 23:4). Jude explicitly points to this when he says that the false teachers have 'abandoned themselves for the sake of gain to Balaam's error'. The motivation behind their actions is greed and its consequence is self-abandonment. It is striking to see how often the tempting allure of money and material prosperity is mentioned in Scripture. Jesus speaks of it as being the major rival to God in the mastery of our lives (*Matt.* 6:24), and compares it to the thorns and thistles that choked the growing seed in the parable of the soils (*Matt.* 13:22). Elsewhere, Paul alerts Timothy, his young ministerial colleague, to its dangers (*1 Tim.* 6:3–10). Greed is a force to be reckoned with and it will assume the most pious of guises to satisfy its yearnings.

Jude's third point of comparison in his exposé of the false teachers is the rebellion of Korah. It was Korah, Dathan, and Abiram who instigated a major challenge to the authority of God's appointed leader of the Israelites, Moses (*Num.* 16:1–3). In doing so, they were not merely seeking to usurp the authority of Moses, but the authority of God himself, and to assert their own authority, based on the support of the common people. Although false teachers would rarely be bold enough to claim that they were issuing a direct challenge to God, a quick look at how their authority squares with that of Scripture will soon reveal whether they are under God's rule or not.

Jude pulls no punches in his devastating critique of the false spirituality behind which these men hide. They are 'blemishes on [or, 'reefs in'] your love feasts' (verse 12). The 'love feasts' were the fellowship meals enjoyed by the early believers, which became the setting for the celebration of the Lord's Supper. These love feasts were not only spoiled by the presence of the false teachers, but were endangered by them in the same way that a hidden reef endangers a ship. These people only look after themselves; they have no love or concern for others.

They are 'waterless clouds, swept along by the winds; fruitless trees in late autumn, twice dead, uprooted' (verse 12) – two things that are in effect a contradiction in terms. So it is with people who come in God's name, claiming to bring God's message, but who have nothing from God to offer. Worse than that, they are 'wild waves of the sea, casting up the foam of their own shame' (13). Like deceptively beautiful waves on the seashore that deposit a filthy scum on the beach, these people leave the sickening emptiness of fruitless and ruined lives behind them.

They are 'wandering stars, for whom the gloom of utter darkness has been reserved for ever' (verse 13). Jude may either be saying that they are like planets that wander around the universe, as opposed to those remaining fixed in their orbits, and so are no sure guide for those who navigate by them, or else he is comparing them to 'shooting stars' – tiny particles that blaze spectacularly for a moment, only to vanish without trace for ever. Either way, it is an apt description of those who are guilty of misleading so many. The 'utter darkness' of the 'outer darkness', which Jesus portrays as the horror of hell, is the only place in which they can expect to face eternity, if they do not repent.

It is a simple, but wise, guiding principle in life that we 'should not judge a book by its cover', or 'a sweet by its wrapper'. Appearances can be deceptive and, when it comes to false teachers in the church, we need to get beyond appearances to detect their deeper motivation, and to ask ourselves where their teaching will ultimately take us.

THEIR FATE AND PRESENT SELF-INDULGENCE

It is to the ultimate destiny of these teachers and their disciples that Jude finally turns his attention in this section. Once more he refers to a source outside the Bible, but his message to his readers is shaped by language drawn from Scripture (*Deut.* 33:2). His purpose is to portray the final judgment and the fate of 'the ungodly' and their 'deeds of ungodliness' (verse 15).

The description is stark and its warning clear. There will come a point in time when God's patience finally runs out. It happened in the days of Noah with that primeval portent of the last judgment – the Flood. God looked down on the wickedness of men and said, 'My Spirit will not contend with man forever, for he is mortal' (*Gen.* 6:3, NIV). What followed (after yet another century of patient pleading on God's part through his servant Noah) was universal destruction in the Flood.

Final judgment is the great and sobering reality with which all of us must reckon. Jude's warning to the false teachers and those drawn in by their heresy is that they too must give an account to God. We, too, must give an account to God one day for the teachings and message we choose to believe. Will our beliefs meet with God's approval?

Jude's description of the false teachers seems so clear-cut that we may be tempted to wonder how anyone in the church could possibly fail to identify them. But the threat they pose is often cloaked behind a very plausible appearance of spirituality. This is why Jude pinpoints the tell-tale signs that betray their true identity. They are 'grumblers, malcontents, following their own sinful desires; they are loud-mouthed boasters, showing favouritism to gain advantage' (verse 16). Seen in that light, they suddenly appear as the kind of people who are more common in our churches than we care to admit – almost every congregation has one! Too often they pursue their cause and try to attract the support of others under the pretext of pursuing either a deeper spirituality or a more faithful orthodoxy. Though both objectives are worthy, when pursued as ends in themselves, without reference to God and his Word, or to Christ through whom alone they are obtained, far from being the means of true blessing, they become destructive to the soul.

There is something quite chilling about a section of the Bible like this. It is almost impossible to read it without our blood running cold. But is this not exactly what it was meant to do? Jude is not scare-mongering, neither is he engaging in the character-assassination of those with whom he cannot agree; he is simply declaring the truth. In a way that is perfectly consistent with the rest of God's Word, he is warning those who are spiritual con-artists that it is ultimately God, who does not judge by appearances, but who 'looks on the heart' (*1 Sam.* 16:7), with whom they must reckon. If that is how the Lord judges, then those who are his children must learn to look beyond appearances too.

4

Built for Battle

But you must remember, beloved, the predictions of the apostles of our Lord Jesus Christ. [18]They said to you, 'In the last time there will be scoffers, following their own ungodly passions.' [19]It is these who cause divisions, worldly people, devoid of the Spirit. [20]But you, beloved, build yourselves up in your most holy faith; pray in the Holy Spirit; [21]keep yourselves in the love of God, waiting for the mercy of our Lord Jesus Christ that leads to eternal life. [22]And have mercy on those who doubt; [23]save others by snatching them out of the fire; to others show mercy with fear, hating even the garment stained by the flesh (Jude 17–23).

Jude began his message to the churches with a spiritual call to arms. He has urged his fellow Christians to 'contend for the faith that was once for all delivered to the saints' (verse 3). He has mapped out the battlefield, pointed out the enemy's positions, traits, and tactics, and assured his readers of the God-given guarantees that belong to the faithful. Now he turns to this little army of Christian soldiers and addresses them directly. His concern is to get the Lord's troops ready for the battle.

Jude's message is apt and relevant for Christians living in the Western world. The freedoms we enjoy and the luxuries with which we are surrounded have bred a generation of complacent and apathetic followers of Christ. All too often, churches are run as though they were business corporations and the kind of Christianity they represent is of the cost-free and pain-free variety. This has produced Christians who tend to be 'soft in the middle' and whose gospel has lost its cutting edge. Battles have been fought, but very often on the wrong front and against straw men and perceived enemies rather than the real thing. However, the kind of complacency and ineffectiveness we lament today has been around for a very long time! The church has always been in danger of going to seed – or as Jesus put it, 'losing its saltiness' (*Mark* 9:50). The issues Jude addresses alert us to this danger and enable us to respond in a way that will not only safeguard the gospel, but also preserve the church's effective witness in the world.

It is noteworthy that the tone of Jude's letter changes at this point from warning to exhortation. Like a good doctor, Jude has said to the ailing patient, 'This is what is wrong', and now he says, 'This is the remedy you must take.' He has made his diagnosis of the spiritual malaise of the churches under his pastoral care and now he provides the spiritual remedy that will preserve the spiritual health of the church in the future.

He identifies three main ways in which God's people must be actively preparing for the spiritual battle they are called to fight. They must be –

ALERT TO THE THREAT OF INFILTRATION

The first area links in with the lengthy warnings Jude has given in the preceding verses. He introduces this first set of exhortations by reminding his listeners of the warnings already given by Christ's apostles. The apostles had learned from Jesus that the 'last time' – the time between Christ's ascension and his return – would not be an easy period in which to be a Christian. The church will be under pressure on two fronts: it will be exposed to the threat of persecution from the hostile world around, and in danger of being led astray by false teachers from within its own ranks. This second danger concerned Jude more than the other.

Jude's readers must be alert to the signs of the times foretold by Christ and his apostles. They must view the world around them through the lens of the truths God has revealed to them in his Word. Paying attention to the warnings of the Bible lessens the shock of much of what we see going on, not just in the world, but also in the church, and helps us to believe that God is still in control.

Attention is focused on the presence of 'scoffers' who will follow 'their own ungodly passions' during this period of 'the last time' (verse 18). Far from being shocked and surprised that such people should be found among the ranks of professing Christians, we should be prepared for them. After all, Christ warned his disciples that such would arise within the church.

Jude identifies three character traits of the scoffers that will help us identify them. They are *divisive* ('cause divisions'), they are *'worldly'*, and they are *'devoid of the Spirit'* (verse 19). A moment's reflection on these marks of counterfeit Christianity will show us just how damaging they really are to the gospel.

Divisiveness is the exact opposite of the unity of believers that lies close to the heart of Christ's message. In his high-priestly prayer Jesus could not have more clearly highlighted the vital importance of unity among his people:

> I do not ask for these [my disciples] only, but also for those who will believe in me through their word, that they may all be one, just as you, Father, are in me, and I in you, that they also may be in us, so that the world may believe that you have sent me. The glory that you have given me I have given to them, that they may be one even as we are one, I in them and you in me, that they may become perfectly one, so that the world may know that you sent me and loved them even as you loved me (*John* 17:20-23).

In other words, Jesus was saying that the credibility of the gospel is bound up with the spiritual unity of the church. That explains why Paul is equally strong in the language he uses about the church in his letter to the Ephesians. Having argued that the 'dividing wall of hostility' (*Eph.* 2:14), separating Jewish Christians from their Gentile brothers, has been broken down, he goes on to exhort all Christians to 'spare no effort in preserving the unity of the Spirit in the bond of peace' (*Eph.* 4:3, my translation).

So when people are received into the fellowship of the church in the name of Christ, but then cause *division* within its ranks, alarm bells ought to ring in our ears. Christ's true message will promote real spiritual unity among his people. Though there may be some outward differences among believers (of denomination or culture), nevertheless, the genuine believer will have a deep inward recognition of the Saviour's voice in the Word of God and an instinctive desire to gather together with all who are drawn to it (cf. *John* 10:16).

Jude also says that these people will be '*worldly*'. That is, despite the veneer of their spirituality, the focus of their lives and teaching will be this present world and not God's kingdom. Paul expresses the contrast succinctly to the Colossians: 'If then you have been raised with Christ, seek the things that are above, where Christ is, seated at the right hand of God. Set your minds on things that are above, not on things that are on earth' (*Col.* 3:1–2).

Jude has already exposed the sensuality that characterized both the lifestyle and the teaching of these infiltrators of the Christian church. Here he describes it in terms of worldliness. If 'the world' – as is so often the case in New Testament usage – designates all that is in rebellion against God, then the last place we should expect to find it is in the church! So when we see professing Christians, and especially Christian leaders, pursuing selfish gain and self-fulfilment in the things of this world, we should politely turn aside and walk away.

Not only will these people be worldly and divisive, they will also stand out as those who are '*devoid of the Spirit*'. In part these words echo Jude's devastating description of the false teachers as 'fruitless trees' (verse 12). They show no evidence of the fruit of the Spirit – 'Love, joy peace, patience, kindness, goodness, faithfulness, gentleness, self-control' (*Gal.* 5:22–23). Those who claim to have been born again of the Spirit of God and who come as God's Spirit-anointed messengers ought to bear the marks of a Spirit-filled Christian; they ought to be 'Jesus-like'! These people, however, were not like Jesus. The most basic evidence of a person's having the Holy Spirit is their submission to the lordship of Christ. As Paul told the Corinthians, 'No-one can say, "Jesus is Lord" except in the Holy Spirit' (*1 Cor.* 12:3). There was no evidence of such acknowledgement or submission in the lives of these people.

Troops who are freshly deployed in hostile territory will receive an extensive briefing before being sent out on duty. One of the first things they will be told is of their need to recognize their enemy – especially when he blends into the communities in which the troops will patrol. The same is true in spiritual warfare. Yes, there is an enemy out there in the world; but there is also an enemy within the visible church, which he has infiltrated in order to subvert the truth of the gospel. Every Christian needs to be alert in order to do his duty. Jude's readers must also be –

COMMITTED TO SPIRITUAL EDIFICATION

Defence is important in the battle for the faith, but it is never enough in itself. So Jude calls us to the kind of spiritual disciplines that will build Christians up and equip them for any and every situation they may face. He says, 'build yourselves up in your most holy faith; pray in the Holy Spirit; keep yourself in the love of God, waiting for the mercy of the Lord Jesus Christ that leads to eternal life' (verses 20–21). Here are four things that will make for strong and effective Christian living.

It is interesting to see that 'the faith' for which we are to contend (verse 3) – that body of truth given 'once and for all' to the church – is the 'most holy faith' in which we are to build ourselves up. The only way to defend the gospel is to grow in it as we understand its truths and put them into daily practice in our lives.

Paul speaks of this in more detail in what is effectively his blue-print for a healthy church (*Eph.* 4:1–16). At the end of that great section he says, 'speaking the truth in love, we are to grow up in every way into him who is the head, into Christ, from whom the whole body, joined and held together by every joint with which it is equipped, when each part is working properly, makes the body grow so that it builds itself up in love' (*Eph.* 4:15–16).

Here is body-building at its best. As we are edified in the church, through the Word, in fellowship with Christ and with his people, and as we learn to function in harmony with one another under Christ, the church will be built up in love! Jude will come on to the element of love in this process in a moment, but what he highlights here is how 'the faith' is not only a truth to defend, but also the truth by which we are to live. When we live by it, we maximize its effective-ness. That actually has a significant bearing on the church's witness to the world. Amid all the discussions and debates over how best to do evangelism in today's church, no definition is more helpful than that given by J. I. Packer. He defines evangelism as *'Christians being Christians in the world'*. In other words, if how we live and what we say is controlled and shaped by the truth of the gospel – which ought always to be the case (*Rom.* 6:17) – then our impact for the gospel on those around us will be incalculable.

Clearly such spiritual muscle tone cannot be developed merely by human effort. Hence we are also to 'pray in the Holy Spirit' (verse 20). There is nothing mystical about this statement. All Jude is telling us is that if we are genuine believers, it can only be because we have been born from above through the regenerating work of God's Spirit. We are Christians only because of what God has done *for* us by his Son and *in* us by his Holy Spirit; and not because of anything we have done for him. That being so, it is only because we have 'received the Spirit of adoption as sons' that we are able to cry out [in prayer] 'Abba! Father!' (*Rom.* 8.15). The Holy Spirit, who enables us to pray that very first prayer of faith – 'Lord, save me!' – is the same Holy Spirit who enables us to maintain the faith-sustaining life of prayer.

The importance of prayer in the life of the church cannot be emphasized too much. It is not merely that every Christian desperately needs to maintain a healthy prayer-life in private – following both the example and the instruction of the Lord Jesus – but as churches we need to maintain a healthy prayer-life too. It is clear from the details recorded of the church's early life in the book of Acts, that regular devotion to corporate prayer was a key element in the usefulness and effectiveness of the first Christians in the early days of gospel expansion. Prayer is the most tangible way of expressing to God that without him we can do nothing.

The third element in this spiritual health regime is to keep ourselves 'in the love of God' (verse 21). Although it is true that as subjects in his kingdom we must also keep ourselves under the law of God, never does it take precedence over our need to be kept in the love of God, as far as the teaching of the Bible is concerned. Apart from his love and grace, God's law can only serve one purpose and that is to condemn those who break it. It will fulfil that purpose for those who have never responded to his loving overtures in the gospel. For those who have believed the gospel, however, God's love and God's law go hand in hand. Jesus told his disciples, 'If you love me, you will obey what I command' (*John* 14:15). God's love to us in Christ reminds us that we are more than mere subjects in his kingdom; we are also children in his family. Our prime focus, therefore, will always be on the unimaginable greatness of God's love and grace poured out on us in Christ. It is a love that stretches back into the mysteries of eternity past; it is a love that stretches forward into the gospel certainties of eternity future; but, supremely, it is the love that reaches down to the depths of Christ's anguish on Calvary, demonstrating the lengths to which God's love was willing to go in order to rescue sinners and make them his sons. Such love is the greatest anchor that our faith can know.

All of these ingredients of spiritual strength and vitality are held together as we are daily 'waiting for the mercy of our Lord Jesus Christ that leads to eternal life' (verse 21). At first sight this may seem an unusual turn of phrase, but it ties in with the larger horizons to which Jude is pointing us in these verses. He is talking about the 'last time' – the last great chapter in the history of God's dealings with this world.

He is directing his readers beyond the horizons of the present to the prospect of our eternal future. When that future is finally ushered in on the day of Christ's return, we will receive, Jude says, 'the mercy of our Lord Jesus Christ'. For those who look to him and wait for him by faith, the day of his coming will be a day of mercy, not of wrath. Though this is certainly a warning for those who as yet do not have faith, it is primarily meant as a comfort to Christians who are only too conscious of our weakness and failure.

Just as there is only one way into the family of God – through his mercy and grace in Jesus – so there is only one way to be kept in his family: through that same mercy and grace. As Christians we fail every day. We can never claim to be good enough for God. Even Paul had to dismiss his own righteousness as 'rubbish' (*Phil.* 3:7) for the sake of knowing Christ and the righteousness he alone provides. Therefore, as we live each day waiting for the final display of God's mercy in Christ – purchased in the past and promised for the future – we are set free from our guilt, shame, and sense of condemnation.

When Christians and churches are committed to this kind of spiritual edification, they literally 'shape up' and are equipped and enabled to stand up for him and contend for the faith in a way he has promised to bless. Finally, Jude's readers are to be –

PASSIONATE ABOUT THE NEED FOR RESTORATION

Continuing in the vein of 'mercy', Jude not only speaks of the need for all Christians to 'wait for the mercy of the Lord Jesus Christ', but also to 'have mercy'. He calls for a merciful spirit that will express itself in a number of ways.

First of all, it will be seen in mercy for 'those who doubt' (verse 22). Troubled times in the church have always led to professing Christians being shaken. For some it is a shaking that exposes the falseness of their faith. In our Lord's parable of the soils the rocky ground represents those who hear the Word and make an initial enthusiastic response, but 'when tribulation or persecution arises', fall away because they have no spiritual root in them (*Matt.* 13:20–21). True Christians must show mercy to those who doubt. The fact that their faith has proved false does not preclude them from being brought to true and saving faith later; but that will be influenced to a significant degree by how they are treated by true believers.

Moreover, troubled times in the church have the capacity to shake the faith of genuine Christians – even those who may hold positions of leadership in the church. The Bible gives many examples of God's people struggling with doubt. The Psalmist bares his soul and acknowledges his struggle of faith (*Psa.* 73:1–28), Jeremiah gives us a glimpse of one of the darkest chapters in his own spiritual experience (*Jer.* 20:7–18) and John the Baptist, when he was in prison, even questions whether or not he was right to believe that Jesus was the Messiah God had promised (*Matt.* 11:1–15). How do we treat those who confess to such inward struggles of soul? All too often they have been crushed, not comforted, by the church, and driven to the margins. Someone once said that the church is the only army in the world that shoots its wounded. Jude says, 'Be merciful!'

Furthermore, he adds, 'save others by snatching them out of the fire' (verse 23). This seems to be an allusion to Zechariah – an Old Testament prophecy that Jude alludes to at a number of points in his letter – where it says of Joshua, the high priest, 'Is not this a brand plucked from the fire?' (*Zech.* 3:2). The imagery of Jude's words communicates something of the urgency of what is at stake. When you rescue something from the flames, there is no time for niceties – act first, give your explanations later. Jude is implying that there are times when drastic action is needed in our dealings with others. In particular, he seems to be thinking about true Christians who had been led astray by the false teaching and sensuality that was spreading rapidly through the churches. In such cases, we must rescue first and reason later. How true that is for Christians in every age who are tempted by some doctrinal novelty, or spiritual fad; or, worse than that, who are being morally compromised by the kind of 'Christian' company they keep.

Jude even says, 'to others show mercy with fear, hating even the garment stained by the flesh' (verse 23). Once more this may link into Zechariah's prophecy with its command to give Joshua a completely new change of clothing (*Zech.* 3:3–5) – a picture of the complete spiritual cleansing that is promised by the Lord's salvation. A sinner is not only cleansed and purified in a legal sense through the grace of justification, but also morally and personally through the grace of sanctification. Jude leaves us in no doubt that, on the one hand, this is a corporate responsibility for the whole church and on the other, it is often a messy business with its own snares and temptations – so we pursue it 'with fear'.

Perhaps the thought in Jude's mind here is similar to that ex-pressed by Paul when he tells the Christians at Philippi, 'Therefore, my beloved, as you have always obeyed, so now, not only as in my presence but much more in my absence, work out your own salvation with fear and trembling, for it is God who works in you, both to will and to work for his good pleasure' (*Phil.* 2:12–13). The exhortation is addressed to the church together as a body – sancti-fication is never merely a private and personal matter. It is also to be pursued with an eye to God and to the work he is doing in our lives – that is, with a sense of reverence and awe. Jude's exhortations in this section are both chilling and thrilling: chilling because we are all too aware of the layers of imperfection and failure bound up with the church in its present precarious state in the world; thrilling because of the potential the church has in God's hands. He is well able to display his strength through his people's weakness and use them to demolish Satan's strongholds on every side. But that will only happen as Christians are built up for battle-readiness and as they engage in the fight of faith, not with arrogance, but in humble and trusting dependence on the Lord Jesus Christ.

5

The Glory of the Gospel

Now to him who is able to keep you from stumbling and to present you blameless before the presence of his glory with great joy, [25]to the only God, our Saviour, through Jesus Christ our Lord, be glory, majesty, dominion, and authority, before all time and now and for ever. Amen (Jude 24–25).

Jude began this brief letter by expressing his intention to write a letter outlining the glorious themes of the salvation that the people of God have in common – he wanted the gospel to be the focus of his message. However, he found it more necessary to address the church's pressing need of guarding the gospel and contending for the faith. But as we said at the beginning, glorying in the gospel and contending for its message are not mutually exclusive; this is clearly demonstrated by the note of praise for the wonder of God's great salvation, found at the end of Jude's solemn letter.

We might feel just a little surprised by this exclamation of praise, at least at first glance. Since so much of Jude's letter has been dark and discouraging – exposing the faults and failings of those who were doing so much damage in the church – we might have expected a more gloomy counsel in the letter's closing paragraph. Christians, and even Christian ministers, can easily become prone to pessimism. When they see things going badly wrong in the church, it is all too easy to give up hope and be filled with doubts and fears about the church's future; but such an attitude is to deny the very truths upon which the gospel rests.

Having looked around at the state of the church and looked within at the weakness of the human heart, Jude now bids his readers look

up to their God and Saviour. He turns their gaze upon the greatness
of the Person in whom they have placed their trust and completes
his letter by ascribing glory to the triune God, Father, Son, and Holy
Spirit.

In the face of so many discouragements, Jude reminds us of the
dimensions of Christ's salvation and shows us why we have every
reason to be confident, even in times of adversity and personal
spiritual failure. Salvation does not ultimately depend on us or on
our ability to hold on to God. Rather it rests in the hands of Jesus
and depends on his infinite ability to hold on to us.

Three things come to light as Jude gives God the glory for all he
has done through his Son and promised in the gospel, and for which
God's people have every reason for rejoicing!

SAFETY IN THE PRESENT

Jude's praise is directed towards 'him who is able to keep you from
stumbling' (verse 24). The accent falls on God and his infinite ability.
Much of what Jude has said would make even the strongest believer
tremble; he has spoken about evil powers that are beyond our natural
ability to withstand. The damage being done to the church at that
time was testimony to the evil nature of the enemy who was behind
it. Our instinctive reaction to such factors is to feel dismay. Our
spirits sag because we tend to look at our problems and then at our
own natural resources and abilities. We know that we do not fight
against flesh and blood, but against the dark powers and forces that
subvert the universe (*Eph.* 6:12). We know, too, that our own strength
and resolve are not equal to those of our enemy. Add into this mix
our own frequent failures, and it is easy to become discouraged.

The gospel gives us the antidote. It points us at every turn away
from self to Christ and all that belongs to us through fellowship with
him. Most significantly, it reminds us of all he has promised to do
for us. God has not only begun a good work in our lives, but has also
promised to carry it through to completion on the day of Christ's
return (*Phil.* 1:6). Our hope is set on the promise of God and his
ability to fulfil it completely.

The word Jude uses for 'keep' carries overtones of guarding or
protecting. That is, Jesus will be the supreme guardian of our souls

and we can rest secure in the knowledge that he will allow no harm to befall us. No one and nothing can pluck us from his hand.

What is it that God is able to do for those who trust him? – He is able to *keep us from stumbling*. This is true in two ways.

He is able to keep his true children from falling when others, who are his in name only, are falling all around. There were many who had professed conversion in Jude's day, but, with the passage of time and under the pressure of persecution, they had abandoned the faith and had gone back to their old way of life in the world. The same things had happened during Jesus' earthly ministry. The vast crowds who followed our Lord initially were thinned out as opposition from the religious and political leaders mounted against him. And so it was for Paul and the other apostles too: Paul knew the pain of seeing dear friends profess faith, only to deny it later (*2 Tim.* 4:9–18), and John had to explain why some had left the churches and become 'antichrists' (*1 John* 2:19).

This is a perennial problem for all churches. What Christian has not experienced the pain and perplexity of seeing someone they once thought to be a true brother or sister in Christ abandon their profession and never show signs of spiritual restoration? The Bible warns us about such things; but it also assures those who are genuinely trusting in Christ that he will never let them go.

The other way in which God is able to keep us from falling is by delivering us from the temptations and sins that have been rampant in the church throughout the ages. In the early church false doctrine and moral failure was spoiling the fellowship and damaging the lives of many, and inevitably this was affecting some who were genuine Christians. There have always been true believers who have either drifted doctrinally, or lapsed morally; but Jude says that such spiritual casualties can be avoided.

On the one hand, no Christian should presume he is immune from such temptations. We should look at those who have fallen in some way, not with a critical and condemning attitude, but with one that says, 'There, but for the grace of God, go I!' Paul rightly warns, 'So, if you think you are standing firm, be careful that you don't fall!' (*1 Cor.* 10:12 NIV). We will put no confidence in our own ability. Instead, we will consciously and deliberately look away by faith to the One who does have the ability to hold us up under the pressures of temptation. We will pray the words of the prayer that Jesus taught us: 'Lead us not into temptation, but deliver us from evil' (*Matt.* 6:13); we will follow where he leads; we will avoid those places, people, and things about which he warns us; we will not only say we trust him, but demonstrate that we trust him by sticking close to him at every point on our hazardous journey through this dangerous world.

When we grasp the truth about Jesus, the strength he supplies and the security he provides, we can only be filled with praise. He is worthy of our worship because he alone is able to keep us safe in this present life.

JOY IN THE FUTURE

The horizons of the gospel are not limited to the present, but point ultimately to the future. The promise that we can be kept from stumbling in the present is coupled with the assurance that 'our Saviour' is able 'to present you blameless before the presence of his glory with great joy' (verse 24) in the future.

This promise consists of two elements. The first is that, in Christ, we will be able to stand in the presence of God's glory as those who are *blameless*. The second, which flows from the first, is that we shall stand in his presence *with great joy*.

At the heart of God's good news for sinners is the message that he will justify all who believe in his Son. Although they are sinful by nature, and guilty before the court of heaven, they will be pardoned for their sin, cleansed from their guilt, accepted as righteous in his sight, and so have peace with God (*Rom.* 5:1–2) – all on account of Jesus Christ and his saving work on their behalf.

This is a glorious truth, for the prospect of divine judgment casts a dark shadow over the brightest and best of our achievements in the present. So, to know with certainty today that we will not be condemned in judgment tomorrow is the greatest news a human being can ever hear. However, there is still the problem of our moral and spiritual imperfection in this world. No matter how faithful a Christian may be, there is no such thing as perfection in this life. If the apostle Paul confessed to being a 'wretched man' on account of the sin that continued to dwell in his heart as a Christian (*Rom.* 7:

13–24), how much more will this description be true of all other Christians!

Jude's response is to point out that we will be perfected. On that day, we will have no shame or embarrassment as we stand in God's very presence because there will be nothing sinful to expose in us. Holiness will be perfected in us. God's own likeness, without the slightest blemish, will be perfectly mirrored in our new-found glory.

The greatest heartache that weighs us down in this life is that we constantly fail and fall short of the glory of God. Not a day goes by without our being reminded that we are not what we ought to be. We grieve the Holy Spirit, we hurt our fellow-Christians, we fail to live up to the standards God expects of his children, and we feel miserable as a result. But the gospel gives us a future horizon to fix our eyes upon – one that always casts a glorious light upon the present. This wonderful prospect reminds us that one day – on that great day – God's work in us will be finished and then we will be perfect!

It is little wonder, therefore, that Jude adds that Jesus will escort us into his Father's glorious presence 'with great joy'. There will be pride and pleasure on his part as he displays the fruit of his labour to the Father he loves. Here is the 'joy that was set before him' for which Jesus willingly endured the cross and despised its shame (*Heb.* 12:2). Here is what Isaiah had in mind when he spoke of the Suffering Servant who would 'see of the travail of his soul and be satisfied' (*Isa.* 53:11, KJV). What a thrilling moment it will be when the entire creation will erupt in spontaneous joy and pleasure at the sight of Christ displaying the finished product of his saving work.

But Jude also has in mind the joy of the glorified Christian – those whom Christ has redeemed and now finally restored to all their God-intended splendour. We who are his children will at that moment enter into a degree of joy never known before. Indeed, in God's presence there is fullness of joy and at his right hand there are pleasures forevermore (cf. *Psa.* 16:11). God's whole creation will explode with pleasure!

GLORY FOR ALL ETERNITY

The greatest thing in all of this is that it will never end. This is no fleeting joy. It is no passing experience of spiritual elation, because from that moment onwards, all rebellion will be crushed for ever and God will be acknowledged in his rightful place throughout the never-ending ages of eternity.

The chorus of heaven will be, 'To the only God, our Saviour . . . be glory, majesty, dominion and authority, before all time and now and for ever' (verse 25). What was rightly his 'before all time' will be seen as his 'both now and for ever'.

This will be true, not merely because he is the great Creator-God who first made and then remade the world, universe, and race that bears his image, but because he made, *purchased*, and then remade all this. It is the fact that he is the Saviour-God that makes him worthy of such high honour. It took something more than the exertion of extraordinary divine energy to accomplish this great feat. It required nothing less than extraordinary divine *expenditure*. It is the price that God was willing to pay that reflects the wonder of the final salvation of his people. His loving purpose to save his people from their sins led him all the way to Calvary!

There is no one, or god, like him in the entire universe. It is not just that he is 'the only God' and, therefore, alone deserves to be worshipped and adored, but that no other 'deity' in any other religion has done anything remotely like this to bring deliverance to a lost world. So, among the plethora of world religions, ancient and modern, the message of the gospel calls us to recognize the one true and living God, that we might honour and enjoy him forever.

Jude signs off his letter in the most fitting way imaginable: *Soli Deo Gloria* – To God alone be the glory! Therein lies our hope!

Group Study Guide

SCHEME FOR GROUP BIBLE STUDY
(Covers 13 weeks; before each study read the passage indicated and the chapters from this book shown below.)

STUDY PASSAGE	CHAPTERS
2 PETER	
1. 2 Peter 1:1–4	1–2
2. 2 Peter 1:5–11	3
3. 2 Peter 1:12–21	4
4. 2 Peter 2:1–3	5
5. 2 Peter 2:4–10	6
6. 2 Peter 2:11-22	7
7. 2 Peter 3:1–10	8–9
8. 2 Peter 3:11–16	10
9. 2 Peter 3:17–18	11
JUDE	
10. Jude 1–4	1
11. Jude 5–16	2–3
12. Jude 17–23	4
13. Jude 24–25	5

This Study Guide has been prepared for group Bible study, but it can also be used individually. Those who use it on their own may find it helpful to keep a note of their responses in a notebook.

The way in which group Bible studies are led can greatly enhance their value. A well-conducted study will appear as though it has been easy to lead, but that is usually because the leader has worked hard and planned well. Clear aims are essential.

AIMS

In all Bible study, individual or corporate, we have several aims:

1. To gain an understanding of the original meaning of the particular passage of Scripture;

2. To apply this to ourselves and our own situation;

3. To develop some specific ways of putting the biblical teaching into practice.

2 Timothy 3:16–17 provides a helpful structure. Paul says that Scripture is useful for:

(i)   teaching us;

(ii) rebuking us;

(iii) correcting, or changing us;

(iv) training us in righteousness.

Consequently, in studying any passage of Scripture, we should always have in mind these questions:

What does this passage teach us (about God, ourselves, etc.)?

Does it rebuke us in some way?

How can its teaching transform us?

What equipment does it give us for serving Christ?

In fact, these four questions alone would provide a safe guide in any Bible study.

PRINCIPLES

In group Bible study we meet in order to learn about God's Word and ways 'with all the saints' (*Eph.* 3:18). But our own experience, as well as Scripture, tells us that the saints are not always what they *are* called to be in every situation – including group Bible study! Leaders ordinarily have to work hard and prepare well if the work of the group is to be spiritually profitable. The following guidelines for leaders may help to make this a reality.

Preparation:

1. Study and understand the passage yourself. The better prepared and more sure of the direction of the study you are, the more likely

it is that the group will have a beneficial and enjoyable study.

Ask: What are the main things this passage is saying? How can this be made clear? This is not the same question as the more common 'What does this passage "say to you"?', which expects a reaction rather than an exposition of the passage. Be clear about that distinction yourself, and work at making it clear in the group study.

2. On the basis of your own study form a clear idea *before* the group meets of (i) the main theme(s) of the passage which should be opened out for discussion, and (ii) some general conclusions the group ought to reach as a result of the study. Here the questions which arise from 2 Timothy 3:16–17 should act as our guide.

3. The guidelines and questions which follow may help to provide a general framework for each discussion; leaders should use them as starting places which can be further developed. It is usually helpful to have a specific goal or theme in mind for group discussion, and one is suggested for each study. But even more important than tracing a single theme is understanding the teaching and the implications of the passage.

Leading the Group:
1. Announce the passage and theme for the study, and begin with prayer. In group studies it may be helpful to invite a different person to lead in prayer each time you meet.

2. Introduce the passage and theme, briefly reminding people of its outline and highlighting the content of each subsidiary section.

3. Lead the group through the discussion questions. Use your own if you are comfortable in doing so. As discussion proceeds, continue to encourage the group first of all to discuss the significance of the passage (teaching) and only then its application (meaning for us). It may be helpful to write important points and applications on a board by way of summary as well as visual aid.

4. At the end of each meeting, remind members of the group of their assignments for the next meeting, and encourage them to come prepared. Be sufficiently prepared as the leader to give specific assignments to individuals, or even couples or groups, to come with specific contributions.

5. Remember that you are the leader of the group! Encourage clear contributions, and do not be embarrassed to ask someone to explain what they have said more fully or to help them to do so ('Do you mean . . . ?').

Most groups include the 'over-talkative', the 'over-silent' and the 'red-herring raisers'! Leaders must control the first, encourage the second and redirect the third! Each leader will develop his or her own most natural way of doing that; but it will be helpful to think out what that is before the occasion arises! The first two groups can be helped by some judicious direction of questions to specific individuals or even groups (for example, 'Jane, you know something about this from personal experience . . .'); the third by redirecting the discussion to the passage itself ('That is an interesting point, but isn't it true that this passage really concentrates on . . . ?'). It may be helpful to break the group up into smaller groups sometimes, giving each subgroup specific points to discuss and to report back on. A wise arranging of these smaller groups may also help each member to participate.

More important than any techniques we may develop is the help of the Spirit enabling us to understand and to apply the Scriptures. Have and encourage a humble, prayerful spirit.

6. Keep faith with the schedule; it is better that some of the group wished the study could have been longer than that others are inconvenienced by it stretching beyond the time limits set.

7. Close in prayer. As time permits, spend the closing minutes in corporate prayer, encouraging the group to apply what they have learned in praise and thanks, intercession and petition.

STUDY 1: 2 Peter 1:1–4

AIM: To appreciate the importance of finding certainty in life and to see how that certainty is only truly found in the salvation God provides through Jesus Christ.

1. In what ways can our need for certainty be a problem, not just in the secular world, but also in the church today? In the light of

what you have read in the introduction to this commentary and what is said at the start of the first chapter, how does this relate to the situation facing Christians in Peter's day?

2. How does Peter use a familiar form of greeting in his letter to establish his credentials to address the problems the church was facing at that time? Why is this important for its relevance to the church in all ages?

3. In verse 1, Peter talks about his readers having 'a faith of equal standing with ours'. What does he mean by that and why does it matter? In what ways can Christians think they have a faith that is inferior to others and how is that problem remedied?

4. What is Peter's prayer for his readers in verse 2 and how does his prayer have a bearing on what they were facing in their Christian experience?

5. Why might it sound strange to our ears for Peter to start this letter by talking about God instead of talking directly about the problems his readers were facing? In what way is his approach both necessary and wise?

6. Looking at verse 4, what does Peter identify as our greatest need as human beings in terms of what we need to be saved from and what we need to be saved for? How do you think this relates to the 'felt needs' that are so common today?

7. How does God meet both aspects of that need through Jesus Christ (verse 3)? What does this teach us about where the Christian life begins? What does it teach us about how the Christian life continues?

8. What reason do we have for being sure that we can benefit from something that happened almost 2,000 years ago?

For STUDY 2: Read 2 Peter 1:5–11 and chapter 3 of the commentary.

STUDY 2: 2 Peter 1:5–11

AIM: To understand the vital importance of spiritual growth in our Christian experience and see what it entails and the impact it makes on ourselves and others.

1. Why is 'growing up' so important for us, not just in our natural human development, but especially in our spiritual experience?

2. How do the words, 'For this very reason . . .' (1:5), in Peter's introduction to this next section, help us to understand what he goes on to say? Why do you think this is especially significant in the face of much of the popular Christianity we see today?

3. Peter says that we are to 'make every effort' to do certain things as we press on towards maturity in the faith (1:5). Why do you think he says this and how does his exhortation match up to what is so often the reality for many of us as Christians?

4. Go through each of the ingredients for spiritual growth that are listed (1:5–7), explain what it means, and discuss what is involved in putting it into practice in your life.

5. If we follow Peter's directives, what difference will it make to us positively in our Christian experience (1:8)?

6. If we fail to heed what Peter is saying, what are the negative implications (1:9)? How does his careful choice of words in this verse shed light on where the obstacles to spiritual progress are usually found?

7. What is involved in making 'our calling and election sure' (1:10)? Why is this so vitally important for everyone, but especially for those who profess to be Christians?

8. Peter sets our sights on the future as the supreme motive for what we do with our lives in the present (1:11). How does this affect your attitude to yourself and how you frame your own life here and now, and how does it change how you relate to others?

For STUDY 3: Read 2 Peter 1:12–21 and chapter 4 of the commentary.

STUDY 3: 2 Peter 1:12–21

AIM: To see that the faith we are called to exercise in response to the gospel is not a 'leap in the dark', but rather a most reasonable thing for us to do.

1. We often hear people object to the gospel by saying, 'But that's just your opinion!' Why is this a question we need to take seriously? How do you think it may have been a question that was troubling Christians in Peter's day?

2. Peter does not doubt the fact that his readers are well aware of the things he has been teaching already (1:12–13). Why then does

he want to remind them of them? Why do we also need reminders and where can we find them?

3. What three reasons does Peter give for needing to issue this reminder (1:13–15)? How do they affect, not just the original readers of that time, but all Christians since then?

4. How does Peter answer the charge that his message (the message of the gospel) is 'myth' (1:16–18)? What does this teach us about the character of the gospel and how does it mark it out as being radically different from other spiritual messages?

5. In what way does the testimony of Peter and his fellow-apostles have implications for how we view the message of the Old Testament (1:19)? What difference should that make to the way we read the Scriptures and how we wait for its fulfilment?

6. What does Peter say about the way the Scriptures came into being? How does this help us appreciate both the human and the divine characteristics of the Bible?

7. How do Peter's teaching and the reasoning that lies behind it give us every reason for confidence in the message of the Bible?

For STUDY 4: Read 2 Peter 2:1–3 and chapter 5 of the commentary.

STUDY 4: 2 Peter 2:1–3

AIM: To appreciate the very real threat posed to the church in every generation by the influence of false teachers and understand how best to guard the church against them.

1. Why are apathy and complacency so damaging to our Christian life personally and the life of the church generally? What reason do we have for thinking these were very real problems in the churches Peter was addressing?

2. In what way does Peter link what he says at the start of this chapter with what he has been talking about at the end of the first? What point is he impressing on all his readers?

3. How does Peter's lesson about what happened in the past through the influence of false prophets help us to appreciate the importance of understanding at least some church history?

4. What do we learn about the way false teachers operate and the effect their teaching has on themselves and those they influence

(2:1)? How can we be alert to such subtlety without being paranoid and always on the defensive?

5. Why are good people so easily taken in by false teachers and their message (2:2–3)? What clues do we see in their lifestyles that indicate that their teaching is out of step with the message of the Bible? Where does this influence ultimately lead?

6. In what way are such ministries often manipulative (2:3)? How would you counsel a young Christian who was being influenced by this kind of teaching?

7. What does Peter say about the fate of false teachers (2:3)? Why should that make us appreciate the importance of sound teaching more fully?

For STUDY 5: Read 2 Peter 2:4–10 and chapter 6 of the commentary.

STUDY 5: 2 Peter 2:4–10

AIM: To recognize the characteristics of false teachers and false teaching, appreciate where their danger lies and see at the same time how God is gracious even when such damaging influences are at work among his people.

1. What happened to the angels who rebelled against God in the past (2:4)? How does their fate serve as a graphic warning to men and women who dare to challenge God's authority – especially if they occupy positions of influence and instruction?

2. How does the flood in Noah's day add weight to the first example and the warning it carries (2:5)? What additional details does it put into the picture?

3. Sodom and Gomorrah are synonymous with the idea of divine judgment. What relevance did they have to the world and even the church of Peter's day? Do they have anything to say to the church and world of our own day?

4. Habakkuk tells us that the God of the Bible is the God who 'in wrath remembers mercy' (*Hab.* 3:2). How is that apparent in what Peter says here (2:5, 7–10)? Why should that give us hope, even when the state of the church seems to be at its lowest ebb?

5. What surprising light does Peter shed on Lot and the way he felt while he lived in Sodom (2:7–8)? What does that say to us about

how a genuine Christian – no matter how weak in the faith – will feel and act in an ungodly society?

6. Why should we be concerned as Christians when we reach a stage in life where nothing shocks us any more? What is the remedy for such indifference?

For STUDY 6: Read 2 Peter 2:10–22 and chapter 7 of the commentary.

STUDY 6: 2 Peter 2:10–22

AIM: To see in greater detail why false teachers who, at face value may sound and seem plausible, are actually far-removed from what is truly Christian and why it is so important for the church to guard against them.

1. It is never a pleasant thing for us as Christians to dwell on things that we know to be wrong. Why, then, does Peter do so at such length in these verses? How does this tie in with the teaching of Jesus?

2. What is it about the attitude of such false Christians to others – particularly those in authority – that alerts us to there being something badly wrong with their understanding of the gospel (2:10–11)? Why is this especially pertinent to the spirit of the age in which we live?

3. Where do their controlling motives lie and where will they ultimately lead (2:12–13)? How does that help us to evaluate the maxim by which so many people live: 'If it feels good, do it!'?

4. How does Peter elaborate on this in what he says in his next statement (2:13–14)? Think of ways in which professing Christians can become 'blots and blemishes' on the character and fellowship of the church.

5. Peter uses Balaam as an illustration of what such people are like and how they operate (2:14–15). What light does Balaam shed on this problem? How was Balaam brought to his senses (2:16)? How might such people be made to face their folly today?

6. How does Peter demonstrate that even though such teachers make great promises, they cannot actually deliver on their claims (2:17–19)? In what way does this tie in with Paul's injunction to Timothy as a true pastor-teacher (*1 Tim.* 4:16)?

LET'S STUDY 2 PETER AND JUDE

7. How does Peter expose not only the error, but also the ugliness and terrible danger of the kind of teaching that was becoming so popular in his day (2:20–22)? Do you think he is overstating the case, or does his warnings still hold true?

For STUDY 7: Read 2 Peter 3:1–10 and chapters 8 and 9 of the commentary.

STUDY 7: 2 Peter 3:1–10

AIM: To appreciate the different mindset the gospel gives the Christian and especially to see how that changes the way we view the future and the prospect of the Lord's return.

1. Why is Peter concerned about his readers' minds and the way they think (3:1)? How does this tie in with Paul's teaching about the new mindset the gospel gives us (*Rom.* 12:1–2)? In what way should that make a difference to the way Christians think as compared to their unconverted friends and neighbours?

2. Where does Peter point to provide the ultimate reference point by which to understand the world, history, and the passage of time (3:2)? How might our appreciation and application of the Bible's message be dulled or damaged?

3. Why should Christians not be surprised by the fact that there are many who ridicule the idea of a personal return of the Lord Jesus Christ (3:3)? How do 'scoffing' and 'following their own sinful desires' go hand in hand?

4. How does Peter outline and then answer their objection to the idea of Christ's second coming (3.4–7)? What does this tell us about the way people are inclined to think naturally and how we are trained to think differently by the gospel? How might this help young people heading off to college or university?

5. What light does the Bible shed on God and his relationship to time, and how does this change our perspective of time and history (3:8)?

6. How does Peter go on to explain the apparent delay in God's fulfilling the promise that his Son would one day come back (3:9)? What are the implications for this first of all for those who are not Christians, then for those who are?

7. What does Peter say about how the world as we know it will end and how that end will come (3:9–10)? How should that affect the way we view the present world and understand the passage of time?

For STUDY 8: Read 2 Peter 3:11–16 and chapter 10 of the commentary.

STUDY 8: 2 Peter 3:11–16

AIM: To realize that, for Christians, the prospect of what God has revealed about the future must make a world of a difference to the way we live in the present.

1. Think of some everyday examples of how the prospect of a future day can make a huge difference to the way we use the time leading up to it. How does Peter use this kind of reasoning to apply what he is teaching about the end of the world (3:11)?

2. According to Peter what kind of things should characterise our lives if we live them in the light of the day of Christ's return (3:11–12)? In what sense can it be said that by living like that, Christians not only wait for, but also 'hasten' the coming of that day?

3. Why does Peter call it 'the day of God' (3:12)? What will this day mean negatively for the world as we know it?

4. What can we learn about the kind of world that will replace the present order of things (3:13)? How should our knowledge of the new world be an encouragement to us in the pain and perplexity of our present experience? Should this have an impact on how we preach the gospel?

5. How does Peter press home the urgency of this strand of Bible teaching (3:14)? Why should this put the need for holiness high on the agenda for both the individual Christian and the church?

6. What does Peter mean when he says, 'Count the patience of the Lord as salvation' (3:15)? How should that affect us in practice?

7. Peter acknowledges that what the Bible says about the end of the world is not easy to understand (3:15–16). How can that lead people to distort what it actually says? Why is it so important that we stay within the limits of what the Bible actually teaches? Does this help us in any way to cope better with the range of teachings Christians hold to on this subject?

For STUDY 9: Read 2 Peter 3:17–18 and chapter 11 of the commentary.

STUDY 9: 2 Peter 3:17–18

AIM: To realize that this is the great climax of all that Peter says in this letter and that the maturity and stability of which he speaks are the great need for Christians in every generation.

1. Can you see any hint that what Peter says to his readers in these verses reflects on his own experiences and failures at an earlier stage in his own life? In what ways does God use failure in the Christian life to bring blessing to his children?

2. What does Peter tell his readers to be on their guard against (3:17)? What is it about false teachers that make them dangerous? Why is instability such a threat to our Christian experience?

3. What can we learn from the verb form Peter uses in his closing command (3:18)? How does it help us guard against a wrong view of progress in the Christian life?

4. What does it mean to grow 'in the grace of the Lord Jesus Christ' (3:18)? How does that work itself out in practice?

5. What does it mean to grow 'in the knowledge of the Lord Jesus Christ' (3:18)? How does that work itself out in practice?

6. How does the closing doxology of this letter provide an extremely fitting climax and conclusion to all that Peter has been saying (3:18)? Why is it true that 'Man's chief end is to glorify God and enjoy him forever'? In what way does this ultimately affect our well-being as God's creatures?

7. What one thing has made the biggest impression on you as you have worked through the teaching of this letter?

For STUDY 10: Read Jude 1–4 and chapter 1 of the commentary on Jude.

STUDY 10: Jude 1–4

AIM: To identify as best we can who Jude is, why he introduces himself as he does, and what his aims are in writing this brief but punchy letter.

1. Assuming that the Jude who introduces himself in these verses is the half-brother of Jesus, why do you think he describes himself as he does in the opening sentence (1)? How does this actually lend weight to what he goes on to say?

2. In what way does the greeting he gives to his readers immediately begin to minister to them in the difficulties they faced (1)? How do these three great facts about what makes a person a Christian continue to be a source of tremendous encouragement in the struggles of the faith?

3. Why are 'mercy, peace, and love' so vital to our Christian experience (2)? Why do you think Jude prays that they might be 'multiplied to you'? How might the same be true for all of us in the Christian life?

4. Jude says that his initial desire was to write about 'our common salvation', but instead he writes to urge his readers 'to contend for the faith that was once for all delivered to the saints' (3). Why do you think this shift in focus was necessary?

5. What does he mean by 'the faith'? Why is it significant that it is the faith 'once for all delivered to the saints? What is involved in contending for the faith?

6. Who are the people Jude identifies in verse 4 and why are they a source of concern for Jude? Why is their influence so subtle and why should Christians in every generation continue to share Jude's concern?

7. Why should there be no contradiction between being a gracious Christian and courageously contending for the gospel of Jesus Christ? How can Christians become imbalanced by leaning too far towards one or other of these positions?

For STUDY 11: Read Jude 5–16 and chapters 2 and 3 of the commentary on Jude.

STUDY 11: Jude 5–16

AIM: To appreciate the warnings Jude issues from God's past dealings with those who deviated from his ways and to recognise the marks of such deviation in the present.

1. There is obviously a sense in which Jude uses the word 'remind' (5) in the sense of 'do not forget'; but, seen in the light of wider

biblical usage, what other emphasis is he bringing out? Why should this be an important element in how we frame our Christian lives?

2. What is striking about the way Jude describes the Exodus (5)? How should that affect the way we view the visible church?

3. How does the rebellion of angels in heaven and the particular sin with which they are charged (6) help us to see the kind of subversive attitudes that can creep in among God's people on earth? What can we learn from the fate of these fallen angels?

4. What were the sins that brought Sodom and Gomorrah their notoriety (7)? Given the sensuality of our modern world, how should this put us on the alert?

5. As Jude links lessons from the past to the kind of people who were destabilising the church in the present, what does he point to as the source of their authority (8)? Why is this so appealing and why is it so dangerous?

6. How does the dispute between Satan and the archangel Michael help us to see where false teachers overstep their limits when it comes to their attitude to different forms of authority (9–10)? How might this be a problem in churches today?

7. What does Jude mean by each of these examples: 'the way of Cain', 'the error of Balaam', and 'Korah's rebellion' (11)? How do they put us on notice to look out for the same kind of things in ourselves, as well as in those who seek to influence the church?

8. How does Jude expose the emptiness of such people in the church of his day (12)? Why do Christians need to beware of succumbing to their influence (13)?

9. Where does the behaviour of such people finally lead (14–15)? How should the traits that distinguish them make every Christian conscious of how easy it is to behave in the very same way (16)?

For STUDY 12: Read Jude 17–23 and chapter 4 of the commentary on Jude.

STUDY 12: Jude 17–23

AIM: To understand that Christians are called to spiritual warfare and how to prepare ourselves to be ready for it.

1. In what way should the predictions given by the apostles help us to make sense of some of the perplexing things that happen in

the church (17–18)? Why was this important in the spiritual climate Jude was facing in the early church? Why does it continue to be true today?

2. Why do you think that references to 'ungodly passions' (18) etc. seem to crop up with such frequency in these two letters?

3. What three things does Jude point to that help us identify the kind of people who would blow us off course in the Christian life (19)?

4. By way of contrast, how should those who are true followers of Christ behave and respond to the damaging influences they find in the church (20)?

5. What is involved in building ourselves up in the most holy faith (20)? How does this tie in with similar instruction given by Paul to the Ephesians (*Eph.* 4:11–16)?

6. What does it mean to 'pray in the Holy Spirit', 'keep yourselves in the love of God', and 'wait for the mercy of our Lord Jesus Christ that leads to eternal life' (20–21)? How should these disciplines be worked out in the corporate life of the church?

7. How should we respond to Christians who fall into temptation and sin (22–23)? How does this reflect the attitude of Christ himself?

For STUDY 13: Read Jude 24–25 and chapter 5 of the commentary on Jude.

STUDY 13: Jude 24–25

AIM: To see how only the glory of the gospel allows us to live in the way Jude describes and how that, in turn, it redirects our lives towards the glory of God.

1. How does Jude's concluding words bring us back to his original intention declared in verse 4 (24–25)? Why must it always be the case that the great truths of what God has done for us underpin what he calls us to do for him?

2. In a situation in which many dear Christians were stumbling and falling spiritually and morally, where does Jude direct his readers for the source of their security (24)? Why must this always be to the fore in our self-understanding as believers? How does it affect our present experience in this world?

3. What is God's ultimate purpose for his people in salvation (24)? Why is it so important to keep in mind where our destiny lies in God's purpose for us in his Son?

4. How does the prospect of the future joy promised in heaven affect our expectations in the kind of joys we experience on earth (24)? What does this say to people who live mainly for pleasure in the present?

5. Why does Jude highlight the uniqueness of the God of the Bible in the form of words he uses here (25)? How does the God of the Bible differ from the gods of other religions and faiths you are aware of?

6. Why is the greatest glory given to God the Father through Jesus Christ his Son (25)? What does this mean for the centrality of Christ in our understanding of the Christian life?

7. What light do the particular qualities of 'glory, majesty, dominion, and authority' shed on the everlasting glory of Christ, both now and in the world to come (25)?

8. How have your studies in 2 Peter and Jude made a difference to the way you view yourself and the way you view your church?

FOR FURTHER READING

JOHN BENTON, *Slandering the Angels: The Message of Jude* (Evangelical Press, 1999).

JOHN CALVIN, *Commentaries*, vol. 22 (Baker Book House, 1979).

PAUL GARDNER, *2 Peter and Jude* (Christian Focus, 1988).

MICHAEL GREEN, *2 Peter and Jude* (Inter-Varsity Press, 1983).

S. J. KISTEMAKER, *James and the Epistles of John, Peter and Jude* (Baker Book House, 1996).

D. M. LLOYD-JONES, *Expository Sermons on 2 Peter* (Banner of Truth, 1983).

R. C. LUCAS & C. GREEN, *The Message of 2 Peter and Jude* (Inter-Varsity Press, 1995).

MARTIN LUTHER, *Commentary on the Epistles of Peter and Jude* (Kregel, 1982).

THOMAS MANTON, *Jude* (1658; repr. Banner of Truth, 1958).

DOUGLAS MOO, *2 Peter and Jude* (Zondervan, 1996).

ALEXANDER NISBET, *1 & 2 Peter* (1658; Banner of Truth, 1982).